STUDIES IN ECONOMIC HISTORY

This new series, specially commissioned by the Economic History Society, focuses attention on the main problems of economic history. Recently, there has been a great deal of detailed research and reinterpretation, some of it controversial, but it has remained largely inaccessible to students or buried in academic journals. This series is an attempt to provide a guide to the current interpretations of the key themes of economic history in which advances have recently been made, or in which there has been significant debate.

Each book will survey recent work, indicate the full scope of the particular problem as it has been opened by research and distinguish what conclusions can be drawn in the present state of knowledge. Both old and recent work will be reviewed critically but each book will provide a balanced survey rather than an exposition of the author's own viewpoint.

The series as a whole will give readers access to the best work done, help them to draw their own conclusions in some major fields and, by means of the critical bibliography in each book, guide them in the selection of further reading. The aim is to provide a springboard to further work and not a set of prepackaged conclusions or short cuts.

STUDIES IN ECONOMIC HISTORY

Edited for the Economic History Society by M. W. Flinn

PUBLISHED

IN PREPARATION

The Decline of Serfdom in Medieval England

Prepared for
The Economic History Society by

R. H. HILTON

Professor of Medieval Social History
University of Birmingham

MACMILLAN

ST MARTIN'S PRESS

First edition 1969
Reprinted 1970

Published by
MACMILLAN AND CO LTD
London and Basingstoke
Associated companies in New York Toronto
Dublin Melbourne Johannesburg and Madras

SBN (paper) 333 10117 0

Printed in Great Britain by
ROBERT MACLEHOSE AND CO LTD
The University Press, Glasgow

Other books by the same author
Economic Development of some Leicestershire Estates in the
Fourteenth and Fifteenth Centuries
A Medieval Society: The West Midlands at the End of the
Thirteenth Century

With H. Fagan
The English Rising of 1381

Edited by the same author
Ministers' Accounts of the Warwickshire Estates of the Duke of
Clarence
The Stoneleigh Leger Book

Contents

Acknowledgements

To Drs Marie Clough, R. J. Faith, I. J. E. Keil, J. Z. Titow and Mrs J. A. Brent, Mr E. J. King and Mr E. K. Vose for permission to quote from their unpublished work (see Bibliography).

To Mr C. C. Dyer for lending me his transcript of court rolls of the Bishopric of Worcester.

To Professor H. A. Cronne and Miss J. R. Birrell for reading and commenting on the work.

Preface

SO long as the study of economic history was confined to only a small group at a few universities its literature was not prolific and its few specialists had no great problem in keeping abreast of the work of their colleagues. Even in the 1930s there were only two journals devoted exclusively to this field. But the high quality of the work of the economic historians during the inter-war period and the post-war growth in the study of the social sciences sparked off an immense expansion in the study of economic history after the Second World War. There was a great expansion of research and many new journals were launched, some specialising in branches of the subject like transport, business or agricultural history. Most significantly, economic history began to be studied as an aspect of history in its own right in schools. As a consequence, the examining boards began to offer papers in economic history at all levels, while textbooks specifically designed for the school market began to be published.

For those engaged in research and writing this period of rapid expansion of economic history studies has been an exciting if rather breathless one. For the larger numbers, however, labouring in the outfield of the schools and colleges of further education, the excitement of the explosion of research has been tempered by frustration caused by its vast quantity and, frequently, its controversial character. Nor, it must be admitted, has the ability or willingness of the academic economic historians to generalise and summarise marched in step with their enthusiasm for research.

The greatest problems of interpretation and generalisation have tended to gather round a handful of principal themes in economic history. It is, indeed, a tribute to the sound sense of economic historians that they have continued to dedicate their energies, however inconclusively, to the solution of these key problems. The results of this activity, however, much of it stored away in a wide range of academic journals, have tended to remain inaccessible to many of those currently interested in the subject. Recognising the need for guidance through the burgeoning and confusing literature that has grown around these basic topics, the

7

Economic History Society decided to launch this series of small books. The books are intended to serve as guides to current interpretations in important fields of economic history in which important advances have recently been made, or in which there has recently been some significant debate. Each book aims to survey recent work, to indicate the full scope of the particular problem as it has been opened up by recent scholarship, and to draw such conclusions as seem warranted, given the present state of knowledge and understanding. The authors will often be at pains to point out where, in their view, because of a lack of information or inadequate research, they believe it is premature to attempt to draw firm conclusions. While authors will not hesitate to review recent and older work critically, the books are not intended to serve as vehicles for their own specialist views: the aim is to provide a balanced summary rather than an exposition of the author's own viewpoint. Each book will include a descriptive bibliography.

In this way the series aims to give all those interested in economic history at a serious level access to recent scholarship in some major fields. Above all, the aim is to help the reader to draw his own conclusions, and to guide him in the selection of further reading as a means to this end, rather than to present him with a set of pre-packaged conclusions.

University of Edinburgh　　　　　　　　　　　　　M. W. FLINN
Autumn, 1968　　　　　　　　　　　　　　　　　　　*Editor*

Abbreviations
Ag.H.R.	*Agricultural History Review*
Ec.H.R.	*Economic History Review*
E.H.R.	*English Historical Review*
V.C.H.	*Victoria County History*
T.R.H.S.	*Transactions of the Royal Historical Society*

The Early History of Medieval Serfdom in Europe

IN the long history of pre-industrial societies one of the constant features has been the existence of social groups whose members were unfree. The freedom which they lacked was not, of course, an absolute quality of social existence. It is a truism which needs no elaboration that in most societies men's freedom of action is limited by the authority of the state, by the power of the rich and by the customary pressures of social groups. And, just as there were always numerous variations in the opportunities, that is the freedoms, of men who were called free, there were similarly many variations in the forms of unfreedom. The view expressed in a Carolingian capitulary that *non est amplius nisi liber et servus*[1] might have been convenient for the serf-owners, but at that particular time completely misrepresented the great complexity of contemporary social conditions. Yet the complex variations in the grades of unfreedom that were to be found in ancient, medieval and later societies should not lead us to minimise the fact of unfreedom for many human beings, often the majority, in these societies. Even if we ignore the limitations on freedom resulting from the poverty, lack of opportunity, lack of influence and lack of power which has always been the lot of most men and women, we could not ignore the fact that, in medieval as well as in ancient societies, these practical limits on freedom were openly institutionalised as hereditary juridical servitude.

Hereditary servile status in medieval Europe was the lot, by and large, of the bulk of the peasantry. There were also unfree persons in administrative posts (*ministeriales*) and in industrial occupations, but these were a small minority of the total servile population and need not be considered here. The term normally employed by modern historians for unfree peasants is 'serfs', although many other terms were used in different countries and at different times during the European Middle Ages. The word distinguishes this social type from the slave, a usage which is paradoxical since the word 'serf' comes from the Latin *servus*,

[1] 'there is none other than free or serf': M. Bloch, *Mélanges Historiques* I (1963) p. 438. It was also a Roman law maxim.

'slave', while the word 'slave' is thought to have been derived from the fact that the early medieval (as distinct from the ancient) slave trade was to a considerable extent supplied by the Slavonic victims of the eastward expansion of the Germans, who sold their captives in western slave markets.

Although some slaves in antiquity were by no means completely without property, the distinction between slaves and serfs is based on the fact that, on the whole, slaves were the chattels of their masters, employed as instruments of production in agriculture or industry, receiving food, clothing and shelter from the master and possessing nothing. Since the medieval serfs were mostly peasants, their actual material conditions were quite different in that they possessed, even if they did not own, the means of production of their own livelihood. These means of production were the farm buildings, agricultural equipment, lands and common rights that made up the peasant holding. The peasant families might have received these as grants from a landowner, who thus became the peasants' lord, but they are just as likely to have possessed them from time immemorial, before falling under the domination of a lord who used his power to establish legal ownership of the peasants' lands.

The early history of medieval serfdom is very complex. In all of the European countries this complexity is reflected in the varied nomenclature of the servile peasant class, as used more particularly in private documents of the period up to the twelfth century. Some peasants were descended from the *coloni* of the late Empire, who, whatever legal disabilities and encumbrances they might have suffered, were not then classed as slaves, but sank into serfdom under the heavy weight of the obligations imposed on them by the estate owners and the state. In so far as the estate structure of the late Empire persisted into the barbarian successor states, the history of this group was fairly straightforward, for their obligations and disadvantages under Imperial law were much the same as they were to be at the time when the surveys or polyptyques of the big estates in the Carolingian period were drawn up. Other peasants were the descendants of full slaves, some of their ancestors having been slaves under the Roman Empire, others having been enslaved during the wars of the Dark Ages. What distinguished these serfs from their slave ancestors was, of course, the fact that they were now *servi casati*, provided with their own holdings from the landowner's estate.

10

Other medieval peasant serfs were descended from free men who had entered into various forms of dependence under lords. Some gave up their holdings and their status in return for the protection of powerful laymen; others became serfs of the Church for the same reason; others who were landless became serfs in order to acquire a holding. The tendency was, even as early as the tenth century, for the differences within the servile peasant class to be ironed out, though this process of simplification was by no means complete by that date, partly because there were probably still many free peasants yet to be enserfed.

This continuing process of enserfment after the tenth century was partly associated, especially in France and the western parts of the Empire, with the growing strength of private jurisdictions. Some historians have interpreted this development, as far as aristocratic lordship over peasant dependants was concerned, as an addition to the power of landowner over tenant, of the power of *seigneur* over subject, sometimes described as the succession of *pouvoir banal* to *pouvoir domanial*. The relationship of private to public jurisdiction and of feudal potentates to public authority is of course an aspect of this subject into which we shall not enter. But as far as the relationship between estate owners and peasants was concerned, it is thought that one of the most important reasons for this development was economic. In western Europe as a whole, by the twelfth century, lords' demesnes had tended to disintegrate, the traditional peasant tenure (the *mansus*) had become so subdivided as no longer to be recognisable by estate stewards, labour services had practically disappeared and money rents had lost their value. The profitable exercise of private jurisdiction, the exploitation of seigneurial monopolies (of the wine press, the oven, the mill, etc.), the reimposition of certain types of labour service (as a subject's duty rather than as tenant's rent) all had an important financial side for lords whose straight landed income was declining.

Early Serfdom in England

ALTHOUGH there are special features to the agrarian development of medieval England, it should not be imagined that the country was exempt from the general conditions which affected the rest of medieval Europe, especially those parts nearest to it. After all, in common with the whole of western Europe, England had been a province of the Roman Empire and had become a successor state governed by a Germanic aristocracy, with the difference no doubt that the Germanic settlement was denser in England than, for instance, in Gaul. During the Dark Ages there had been abundant contact between the English ruling aristocracies and those of continental Europe, abundant contact between the English Church and Rome, and a volume of trade which had made the fortune of such northern Frankish ports as Quentovic. The almost complete replacement of the Old English by a Norman-French aristocracy (with Flemish and Breton supporters) by the time that 'Domesday Book' was compiled naturally strengthened similarities of social structure, especially since for over a century many English landowners possessed estates in Normandy, and even after the loss of Normandy had direct political contacts with the Continent through Gascony.

In continental Europe by the thirteenth century two different types of division within the peasant class can be seen. First of all there was a division in terms of economic resources, broadly speaking, between those peasants who had sufficient land to feed the family, which demanded the use of a plough and a plough team of oxen or horses (in French, the *laboureurs*), and those who had holdings which were too small for the adequate subsistence of a family, and were cultivated by the spade and the hoe, occasionally by a borrowed plough, and who had to labour for others in order to gain their living (the *manouvriers*). The second main division was in terms of personal status. Apart from such peasants as had retained their free status, the servile peasants were broadly divided into those who were the descendants of slaves (*servi*) and those whose ancestry was not servile in the strictest sense of the word, but whose subordination to their lords was hardly distinguishable in type from that of the true serfs. These were known as the *vileins* in France and the French-speaking parts of the Empire. They were regarded at the time as typical of the peasant class. Their supposed characteristics supplied the courtly *littérateurs* with the adjective *vilein* and the noun *vileinie* to imply everything that was base and opposed to the virtues of chivalry. The two types of division of the peasant class did not necessarily coincide, for well-to-do *laboureurs* could either be *serfs* or *vileins*.

Similarly, in England, by the thirteenth century, there was a recognisable division between the peasants with holdings of twelve to fifteen arable acres (halfyardlanders) or more, and those with small holdings which in a large number of cases must have been under five acres. The former correspond to the continental *laboureurs* and, without necessarily being affluent, had holdings from which a family could be fed. This was not the case with the smallholding cottars who had to find other ways of reinforcing their incomes, including, of course, work for wages on the demesne or on the bigger peasant holdings. The division into free and servile did not correspond to this division. Nor did the division of the servile as between the *nativi* (meaning servile by birth) and the *villani* (not necessarily servile by birth) correspond either to the division of economic resources or (at any rate clearly) to the division which had been visible in the eleventh century between the *servi*, whom we translate as 'slaves' rather than 'serfs', and the *villani*, *cottarii* and *bordarii*, whom we cannot assume to have been legally unfree. The *villani* at any rate are definitely stated, in the treatise known as 'The Laws of Henry I' (*c.* 1120?), to be entitled to the free ceorl's wergild of 200*s*.[1]

The reasons for the difficulty of distinguishing by the thirteenth century between those members of the servile class who were descended from slaves and those who were the descendants of the free villeins of 'Domesday Book' are to be found in the history of the relations between landlords and tenants since the end of the eleventh century. But before we take the history of these two centuries into account, we must remember that slavery

[1] In F. Liebermann (ed.) *Die Gesetze der Angelsachsen* (1903–16) chaps. 70, 76.3a. But this recognition of their freedom did not prevent the author of the *Leges* from describing villeins as *viles et inopes persone* (chap. 29.1a).

13

was an important aspect of the Anglo-Saxon class structure. According to 'Domesday Book', over England as a whole, 9 per cent of the counted population in 1086 were slaves, the proportion reaching 20 per cent or more in the western counties.[1] This is not surprising in view of the frequent references to slavery in the Anglo-Saxon law codes, references which are, however, impossible to use statistically. Many of the slaves enumerated in 'Domesday Book' were clearly counted as part of the demesne resources of landowners: their typical occupation was that of demesne ploughman or oxherd. Such was the ploughman of Ælfric's *Colloquy*, a demesne ploughman rather than a tenant, and not free. But in pre-Conquest England, when men, women and children could be reduced to slavery as a punishment, or sold into slavery because of family poverty, it seems more than likely that there would also be slaves off the demesne, working on the holdings of well-to-do free families. Such slaves might well be ignored by the Domesday Commissioners whose interest was greater in the demesnes than in the tenant holdings. Furthermore, it must be assumed that the same process took place in England as we have seen on the Continent, that is the placing of slaves on holdings (*servi casati*). These may well appear to some extent in 'Domesday Book' as *bordarii*. This process continued in the twelfth century, when the remaining demesne slaves were given holdings as part of the wage for the job, ultimately to be absorbed into the general body of unfree tenants.[2]

There must have been, therefore, a substantial number of the descendants of Anglo-Saxon slaves, *theows*, among the unfree peasants of thirteenth-century England. These could in theory be the *nativi* who are bracketed with the *villani* in many descriptions of estates well into the fifteenth century, or the *nativi de sanguine* who appear in the fifteenth-century court rolls. But this verbal distinction between neifty and villeinage did not amount to very much because the pressure of landowner demand for extra revenue (including extra labour services) from the manorial population resulted in the total confusion of the two, to

[1] F. W. Maitland's *Domesday Book and Beyond* (Cambridge, 1897), now in a paperback edition (1960), is the most easily accessible introduction to Domesday statistics.

[2] On this whole subject, see M. M. Postan, 'The Famulus' (*Economic History Review*, supplement no. 2).

the disadvantage, naturally, of the villein or customary tenant.[1]

Now there seems to be every reason to suppose that long before the Norman Conquest, on English estates as on those of the continental landlords, part of the labour on the demesne was provided by the tenants. Some of these are described in charters, some in the famous *Rectitudines Singularum Personarum* (*c.* 1000).[2] Not much, unfortunately, is known about the scale of demesne cultivation, but it would appear that by the twelfth century in England the same tendency to the disintegration of demesnes was to be found as on the Continent. The evidence for this tendency is mainly from ecclesiastical estates, whose surveys show not only the leasing out of portions of demesne land to tenants, but also indications of forceful pressure by tenants owing labour service to free themselves of this type of rent obligation in favour of money rent. In any case, of course, if demesne areas were being reduced, or leased out *en bloc*, fewer labour services would be needed and the door would be open for tenants to achieve a transformation of their obligations. But it should be emphasised here that the rentals and surveys of the mid-twelfth century which hint at these encroachments also give much detail about the not inconsiderable level of labour rent still remaining. More important, the customary tenants or villeins who owe these labour services are not referred to as servile. They are in fact clearly to be distinguished from the few *servi* or *ancillae* mentioned as such by name. Furthermore these villeins, though owing labour services, are not yet normally further burdened with such obligations as merchet (payment for permission to marry off son or daughter), heriot (death duty), toll (payment for permission to sell livestock) or arbitrary tallage (annual tax). This is significant because on the Continent these were recognised as the hallmarks of serfdom and by the twelfth century

[1] The reappearance of a supposed distinction between the descendants of slaves (villeins in gross) and of ceorls (villeins regardant) in the fourteenth century, with echoes in the sixteenth, is a matter of lawyers' theory rather than of fact. The great mobility of the rural population after the middle of the fourteenth century would add to, rather than diminish, the confusion referred to above. But see I. S. Leadam (ed.) in *Select Cases in the Star Chamber* (Selden Society) II (1911) pp. cxxvii ff.

[2] *English Historical Documents*, II (1953), ed. D. C. Douglas, pp. 813–16.

15

were being demanded of free as well as of servile dependants.

The pressure by tenants in the mid-twelfth century may have partly been helped by economic conditions (a wish for easily realisable cash revenues on the part of estate owners), but it may also have been encouraged by the internal divisions of the ruling class and in particular the vulnerability of the ecclesiastics. The atmosphere seems to have changed considerably with the establishment of the Angevin monarchy, though increasingly abundant documentation may partly be responsible for our impression. We might even speak of a counter-attack by estate owners. The villeinage cases which appear in the records of the 'Curia Regis' from the 1190s onwards show that lords were waging a successful battle against their customary or villein tenants precisely on the question of freedom, freedom being no abstract matter but a question primarily of whether the tenant had a hereditary obligation to do labour services. The judges of the royal courts, on the other hand, were only interested in providing a forum for free tenants and were prepared to abandon customary tenants to the jurisdiction of the manorial courts. The prevailing tone in any case was hostile to customary rights, and it is no wonder that if the kings tried to ride roughshod over the customary rights of their barons, these barons should do the same with their own tenants. In addition there were the same financial difficulties (the price of costly military and social aspirations rising faster than revenues) which encouraged the fiscal exploitation of private jurisdiction on the Continent. We therefore have the paradoxical situation of a monarchy trying to extend its power at the expense of the feudal aristocracy, whilst at the same time abandoning the free but customary villein tenants to their lords, whose private jurisdictions at the manorial level developed strongly, even though their baronial courts withered into insignificance. However, the paradox is more apparent than real, since the king was not only sovereign, but feudal lord of the many customary tenants on the royal demesne. And his justices, too, would all be lords of manors.

When the dust settled down, by the middle of the thirteenth century, the pattern which emerged differed significantly from that of the previous century. Landlords on the whole had resumed the active cultivation of the demesne and were reaping the benefits of rising agricultural prices. In spite of some doubts about the status of free men holding land in villein tenure, the equation was established: villein or customary tenure is servile, villeins are serfs and have no action in the royal courts over rents or services against their lord. Since one of the economic objectives of the lords was to ensure a good supply of tenant labour (even if not always fully used), and since it was not difficult to prove that most customary holdings had in the past owed labour services, these services became a test of villein status. In fact, reading the villeinage cases in the Curia Regis Rolls, one gets the impression that almost any customary peasant obligation was being brought as evidence to prove that tenures and tenants were servile. At the same time, to add good measure, the continental tests for serfdom, such as merchet and heriot, were added to the list of exactions, which at the same time proclaimed that a peasant was a servile villein and increased the lords' revenues from him. Neifty and villeinage were virtually assimilated.[1]

The Significance and Distribution of Free Tenures

THE historical development of customary tenure into servile villeinage, which we have briefly sketched, is, of course, only one aspect of the history of the English peasantry before the end of the thirteenth century. Another aspect was the development at the same time of free tenures. This was partly a consequence of the expansion of cultivation in areas of wood, waste and marsh. New holdings were often held in free tenure, a measure taken by landowners to attract new settlers. This relationship between the assarting of wood and waste and free tenure is a commonplace in western European agrarian history. The growth of free tenures was also partly a continuation of the effort we have already noted in the twelfth century by some of the wealthier tenants to convert their customary holdings and their own personal status.[2]

England shared the general circumstances which lay at the back of this development of free tenure with other countries of western Europe. In some respects the results were similar. The

[1] R. H. Hilton, 'Freedom and Villeinage in England', *Past and Present*, 31 (1965).
[2] E. Miller, *The Abbey and Bishopric of Ely* (1951), pp. 121 ff.; R. H. Hilton, 'Gloucester Abbey Leases in the Thirteenth Century', in *University of Birmingham Historical Journal*, IV (1952).

purchase of freedom by serfs with money was even welcomed as a fiscal device by the French Crown and was systematically exploited.[1] Another feature of the improved status of some western European peasants was the collective acquisition through purchase from their lords of *chartes-lois*, which lightened and defined the obligations of whole communities, mostly of *vileins*, occasionally of *serfs*. In Germany the drawing up of the famous *Weistümer*, without necessarily involving enfranchisement, stabilised to the peasants' advantage their customary rights. In England, however, although the occasional drawing up of manorial custumals in the thirteenth century might be regarded as analogous to the *chartes-lois* and the *Weistümer*, it was the actual growth in the number of free tenants that was the main countervailing tendency to the predominant trend already described – the enserfment of customary tenants. Another special feature of the English situation was that the principal hallmark of servility was by now the performance of heavy labour services, even though merchet, heriot, tallage and other obligations had been added for good measure. On the Continent, the subordination to their lords of both *vileins* and *serfs* was primarily signified by their obligation to pay *formariage*, *mainmorte* and *chevage*. Labour services on the demesne had not been an overriding economic necessity to the lords for many years. This point is worth emphasis in view of the tendency of some English historians to equate serfdom too completely with the performance of labour services.

The curious situation in England at the end of the thirteenth century then was that, while the whole body of customary tenants, or villeins, had been declared unfree, the proportion of free tenants was probably greater in some areas than it had been in 1086. Overall figures which enable comparisons to be made are only available for a few counties, those covered by an inquiry of 1279–80: parts of Huntingdonshire, Cambridgeshire, Bedfordshire, Buckinghamshire, Oxfordshire, Warwickshire and Leicestershire.[2] These counties were probably intermediate in social structure – at any rate as far as the matter of free and villein tenure is concerned – between East Anglia and Lincoln-

[1] M. Bloch, *Rois et Serfs* (1920).

[2] Hunts., Cambs., Beds., Bucks. and Oxon., printed by the Record Commission in *Rotuli Hundredorum*, II (1818); Kineton and Stoneleigh Hundreds, Warwickshire, in Public Record Office, E. 164. XV;

shire, well known for the large numbers of free tenants, and the western counties, also well known for the large numbers of slaves in 1086 and subordinated villeins at later dates. They also contained at the end of the eleventh century fairly average proportions of old cultivated land and woodland available for the expansion of the cultivated area. Hence they are not a bad sample. Except for Leicestershire, where the proportion of sokemen in the two hundreds for which we also have data from 1279 to 1280 was 28 per cent, the highest proportion of freemen or sokemen in 1086 was 4 per cent (Cambridgeshire). By 1279–80 the overall proportion in the area covered by the 'Hundred Rolls' was about 40 per cent free tenants (of whom half were smallholders). This average, of course, conceals local variations. In parts of Cambridgeshire and Bedfordshire between 55 per cent and 70 per cent of the total recorded peasant households were holding in free tenure, whereas in parts of Oxfordshire only about 20 per cent were free tenants.[1] And if we get down to village level, variations in social evolution are even more striking. While in some Leicestershire villages in the two hundreds concerned there was a straightforward growth in the number of free tenants (or sokemen) between 1086 and 1279–80, in others we find sometimes that a small population of serfs, villeins and bordars grows into a much larger population of free tenants (the case of Mowsley), while in other villages the proportion of free tenants decreased (as at Blaby) or even vanished (as at Aylestone).[2]

The balance between villeinage and free tenure can only be guessed at in other parts of the country, because the evidence is fragmentary. As a matter of general principle, it would seem that where peasant assarting was encouraged, free tenures increased in number. On the other hand, areas dominated by big and highly manorialised estates tended to have a high proportion of villeins subjected to the whole range of servile obligations, from heavy labour services to tallage and merchet. These two sets of conditions could of course exist within a few miles of each other,

---

for Guthlaxton and Gartree Hundreds, Leicestershire, see R. H. Hilton, *The Economic Development of Some Leicestershire Estates* (1947) p. 7.

[1] Figures in E. A. Kosminsky, *Studies in the Agrarian History of England in the Thirteenth Century* (1956) pp. 205–6, 228.

[2] *V.C.H. Leics.* II, p. 168.

so that the juxtaposition of tenants of very different juridical status and economic position would add considerably to the tensions in the countryside. Thus the fen-edge villages on the estate of the Lincolnshire Priory of Spalding were subject to heavy villein labour services, while other fenland villages were occupied by almost self-governing communities of free tenants. Suffolk's free population was strengthened as a result of the early industrialisation and commercialisation of the county, but the villeins on the estates of the Abbey of Bury St Edmunds owed considerable servile obligations. Sussex likewise presents a picture of free tenure due to assarting, by the side of heavy villein services on highly organised estates. Villeinage on the estates of the Abbots of St Albans was complicated by the settlement of free *adventitii* from London. The evidence from some lay estates in Hampshire shows an increase in the free population between the end of the eleventh and the end of the thirteenth century, from a negligible amount to a proportion of nearly 30 per cent of the tenant population. On the other hand the overall proportion of free tenants on the Bishop of Winchester's estate was only 5 per cent, though on one village only it was up to 25 per cent. Such examples could be multiplied.[1]

However, in spite of the existence of very diverse tenurial structures within the same area, it is possible to pick out broad regional differences with regard to the greater or lesser incidence of servile conditions. In the far north and north-west, customary tenures predominated, often very ancient in character. The servile nature of Northumbrian dreng and bond tenure is by no means certain, although both were associated with the performance of labour services. But the Northumbrian region was not universally manorialised, so in parts the equation between customary tenure and servitude was vague. On the other hand, the manorialising pressure of the Durham Bishopric and Priory estate administrations resulted in a clearly servile villein population within the Palatinate. The same sort of pressures may have

[1] H. E. Hallam, *Settlement and Society* (1965) pp. 202–6; G. Unwin in *V.C.H. Suffolk*, I; P. Wragge in *V.C.H. Sussex*, II; F. R. H. Du Boulay, *The Lordship of Canterbury* (1966) pp. 173, 183; A. E. Levett, *Studies in Manorial History* (1938) p. 191; V. M. Shillington in *V.C.H. Hants*, V; J. Z. Titow, 'Land and Population on the Estates of the Bishop of Winchester, 1209–1350' (unpublished Cambridge Ph.D. thesis) pp. 97–8.

been at work in Lancashire on the de Lacy estates, for example. Here was villeinage which was equated with servitude, but without heavy labour services, for stock-raising rather than arable farming was the main economic activity. Assarting, in the Forest of Rossendale for example, did not lead to free tenure, but to tenures at will as well as to villein tenures. Freer peasant conditions in Yorkshire, on the other hand, have been shown to be associated with the twelfth-century colonisation of the waste (natural or man-made) but Yorkshire was also a land of feudal and ecclesiastical landownership and of manorialisation (especially in the Vale of York) leading to the development of villeinage.[1]

In those parts of the east Midlands not covered by the 1279–80 'Hundred Rolls' there seems to have been a similar growth of free tenures in the twelfth and thirteenth centuries. This was the case with Lincolnshire, especially in the Fens, though the growth in free tenures did not exclude a parallel development of villeinage, with heavy labour services, on some of the big estates. In Nottinghamshire and Northamptonshire, too, free tenures increased in importance in the twelfth and thirteenth centuries, particularly as a function of peasant assarting of the forests. This was not altogether to the liking of some of the big estate owners. Peterborough Abbey for instance attempted both to buy up freehold land in order to increase the area under demesne, and to control the activity of its villeins who were attempting to enter the freehold property market. The East Anglian counties underwent a different experience from those of the east Midlands. Already in 1086 they had a high proportion of free tenants (nearly 40 per cent). In some cases this may have been reduced by manorialisation, but here the principal counteracting tendency was the general development of production for the market and in particular the industrialisation of many villages. East Anglia like the Home Counties was also strongly affected by the pull of London, a refuge as well as a market, for rural immigration into the capital by the end of the thirteenth century was for the most part from East Anglia. But production for the market could

---

[1] J. E. A. Jolliffe, 'Northumbrian Institutions', *E.H.R.* XLI; F. Bradshaw in *V.C.H. Durham*, II; *Halmota Prioratus Dunelmensis*, ed. W. H. Longstaffe and J. Booth (Surtees Society, 1889) *passim*; A. Law in *V.C.H. Lancs.* II; G. H. Tupling, *The Economic History of Rossendale* (1927) pp. 36–8, 70–1; T. A. M. Bishop, 'Manorial Demesne in the Vale of York', *E.H.R.* XLIX (1934).

strengthen manorial organisation, if estate owners chose to expand demesne production, while village industrialisation could work in the opposite direction. These opposite trends affected East Anglia, Essex and Hertfordshire and the consequent tensions had their outcome in 1381.[1]

Of the areas affected by the development of production for the market, and particularly by London, the more interesting is Kent. This has traditionally been thought of as the home of peasant freedom, whose origins have been pushed back well into the Dark Ages. It certainly seems to be the case that in the thirteenth and fourteenth centuries the relative freedom of tenure in gavelkind, the characteristic form of Kentish customary tenure, was generally admitted. Now this is a very instructive case. Gavelkind was not like ordinary free tenure. There were associated with it in the thirteenth century some incidents elsewhere associated with serfdom. Gavelkind holdings also owed labour services, though these were light and not unlike the boon services owed by some free tenants in other counties. It may be, in fact, that what distinguished Kent from other parts of England where customary tenures developed into servile villeinage was that the rich Kentish peasants were strong enough to reject the exercise of lordship which pushed down their fellows elsewhere. This idea is summarised by a recent writer on Kentish history in the following succinct phrase: 'It may be that the famous Kentish freedom was a thirteenth-century concept which arose from the practical power of Kent landholders to handle their own estates.'[2]

Although there was a clear difference between Kent and Sussex with regard to peasant status, in that Sussex knew no gavelkind and villein servility on manorialised estates was to be found there, this was still a county with considerable numbers of free tenants. These mostly existed as a function of the assarting of woodland. The same conditions were probably true of the Wealden part of Surrey. But as we move westwards we enter areas more com-

[1] A. B. Wallis Chapman in *V.C.H. Notts.* II; E. J. King, 'The Abbot of Peterborough as Landlord' (unpublished Cambridge thesis), chap. IV; *V.C.H. Suffolk*, II; F. G. Davenport, *The Economic Development of a Norfolk Manor* (1906); W. Hudson, 'Traces of Primitive Agricultural Organisation', *T.R.H.S.* 4th ser. I; K. C. Newton, *Thaxted in the Fourteenth Century* (1960); G. Williams, *Medieval London: from Commune to Capital* (1963) pp. 138–40.

[2] Du Boulay, op. cit. p. 138.

pletely dominated by manorialised estates of ancient foundation. Peasant conditions in Hampshire, Berkshire, Dorset, Wiltshire, Somerset and Devon were largely formed under the direct or indirect influence of such estate owners as the Bishops of Winchester and Bath, and the Abbots of St Swithun's (Winchester), Abingdon, Malmesbury and Glastonbury, to mention only the most outstanding. This does not mean that the pressure was unrelieved. In Berkshire there were quite a number of privileged tenants of the ancient demesne of the Crown. We have seen that there were parts of Hampshire where free tenures increased in number in the twelfth and thirteenth centuries, perhaps as a result of assarting, though when assarting was done within the framework of a great estate, such as that of the bishops, it could result in non-customary leasehold rather than free tenures. Even in Devon, with its past history of slavery, there was a growth of free tenures due to assarting, and the development of mining and of new town foundations.[1]

The same overall picture also applies in the west Midland counties. Gloucestershire and Worcestershire were above all areas of big, old, manorialised estates, mostly Benedictine, such as those of the Bishops and Priors of Worcester, and the Abbots of Evesham, Gloucester, Winchcombe and Cirencester (Augustinian). Their influence produced a social structure somewhat different from that of the adjacent central Midland counties of Oxfordshire and Warwickshire where free tenure, though not developed on the same scale as in some of the east Midland counties, was nevertheless of considerable importance. It is true that free tenures were associated with assart lands in such woodland regions as Feckenham Forest in east Worcestershire, but these were a small minority. Then the pattern changes again as we move into the Marcher counties of Shropshire and Herefordshire. To the extent that a substratum of Welsh agrarian custom remained, this could augment the numbers of both free and unfree members of the rural population – there is no lack of evidence for free tenants of Welsh descent. But it may be that the availability of land for colonisation, the strong pastoral element in the economy and the absence of large-scale early manorialisation resulted in a high proportion of free tenants at the end of the

[1] See works cited on p. 20, n. 1 above; J. S. Drew, 'Manorial Accounts of St Swithun's Priory, Winchester', *E.H.R.* LXII; E. C. Lodge in *V.C.H. Berks.* II; H. P. R. Finberg, *Tavistock Abbey* (1951) pp. 68–75.

thirteenth century. Surveys of the manors on the estate of the Bishop of Hereford before 1300 show that nearly 40 per cent of the tenants were holding in free tenure and nearly 30 per cent in burgage tenure. Many of these last must have been in agricultural occupations.[1]

The end of the thirteenth century and beginning of the fourteenth was the time when the situation of the customary tenant was most affected by the servile legal status which had been elaborated in the courts to his disadvantage for over a century. Labour services were at their peak, and it did not matter whether they were performed or temporarily commuted for money (*venditio operum*) as far as the economic burden on the holding was concerned. In addition there was a whole range of monetary exactions, including an element of straight money rent; court amercements; entry fines; tallage; multure. The villein could be made to pay for a licence fee before being allowed to sell any livestock; he would certainly have to pay for permission to marry off a daughter or even a son; his daughter would have to pay a fine if she became pregnant out of wedlock; his heir would have to hand over his best beast or chattel as *heriot* (as well as the second-best beast as *mortuary* to the parson); he was not allowed to buy or sell land without permission; he was not allowed to leave the manor. These were the basic restrictions implicit in villeinage, and there might be more or less depending on local custom. When one considers that free tenants were not only allowed freedom of movement and of the alienation of their property, but (unless they were smallholders) had less rent per acre to pay,[2] the juxtaposition of substantial numbers of them alongside the villein tenants must naturally have affected the attitude of the villeins, and thus the very history of villein tenure and status. The fact that perhaps half of the free tenants, in areas where free tenure was abundant, were poor smallholders does not appear to have affected the desire of often well-to-do villeins to achieve the legal and social advantages of free status.

What is the relevance of this insistence on the existence of a high proportion of peasants holding in free tenure at the very time when the lords and the law courts seemed to have imposed

[1] R. H. Hilton, *A Medieval Society* (1966); 'The Red Book of Hereford', ed. A. T. Bannister, *Camden Miscellany*, xv (1929).

[2] Kosminsky, op. cit., pp. 242 ff.

serfdom both in theory and in practice on the customary tenants? Most interpretations of the end of villeinage in England concentrate only on the history of the villeins themselves. They relate changes in villein status to such impersonal factors as the fall in the population, the changed land-to-labour ratio, the long-term fall in agricultural prices. In so far as they admit that any role was played by the conscious action of the persons and classes involved, it is the decision of the landlords to commute labour services, lease out demesnes and lower the overall total of rent demands which they consider to be alone important. Any action on the part of the peasant, while not ignored, is considered to be irrelevant. A recent writer, for instance, states that 'historians are in general agreement that [the Peasant Revolt of 1381] was a passing episode in the social history of the late Middle Ages' and goes on to say that 'it did very little to speed up and nothing to arrest the general movement towards commutation of labour services and the emancipation of serfs'.[1]

The 1381 revolt, taken in isolation, certainly cannot be seen as the initiating event in the decline of serfdom. It was, in fact, by no means simply a peasants' rising. And as a *peasant* movement it was an end rather than a beginning. For, as can be shown without going much beyond source material in print, smaller-scale peasant risings and other symptoms of unrest had been common since the middle of the thirteenth century.[2] For the purposes of our present argument, the important feature in them was that they frequently involved the claim by the discontented that they were not, and should not be, serfs but free men. For tactical reasons they sometimes made less extensive claims, such as that they were entitled to the treatment of the privileged sokemen of the ancient demesne of the Crown, giving them protection against increased rents and services and certain privileges in real actions analogous to those of free tenure.[3] Now there can be little doubt that this pressure by villein tenants was

[1] M. M. Postan, *Cambridge Economic History of Europe*, I (2nd ed., 1966) p. 610.

[2] R. H. Hilton, 'Peasant Movements Before 1381', in *Essays in Economic History*, II (1962), ed. E. Carus-Wilson.

[3] The problems of ancient demesne are dealt with by P. Vinogradoff in *Villeinage in England* (1892); R. S. Hoyt, *The Royal Demesne in English Constitutional History* (1950); and R. H. Hilton, *The Stoneleigh Leger Book* (Dugdale Society, 1960), introduction.

strengthened by the coexistence with them in the countryside of the large numbers of free tenants and tenants of ancient demesne. The fact that many of the free smallholders had a miserable existence on the edge of starvation is irrelevant. What is an incontrovertible fact is the constant demand for freedom of status, sustained until 1381 and reiterated then when the actual economic advantages of free tenure were by no means so obvious as they had been a century earlier.

Lords' Reactions to Demands for Freedom

IN the long run the lords may have accepted the erosion of servile villeinage. Their immediate reaction to villein claims to what they alleged was a recently lost freedom was usually unambiguous. By the fourteenth century the doctrine of servile villeinage was in general well enough established for villeinage cases in the courts to be arguments on technicalities. In so far as the characteristics of villeinage now appear, those which are mentioned tend to be personal rather than tenurial — merchet and tallage at will usually being emphasised. The legal doctrine was supported by classical as well as medieval social theory which emphasised the natural and divine sanctions for the subordination of serf to lord. The canon of Leicester was echoing the old doctrine when he said of the leader of a group of villeins who asserted their freedom:

> *Quid faciet servus nisi serviet et puer eius?*
> *Purus servus erit et libertate carebit.*

There were other views of course, also ancient. Was William de Herle, advocate of William atte Thorne against Bartholomew Pecche in 1310, briefed by his client, or did he repeat a common-place of lawyers when he said 'in the beginning every man in the world was free and the law is so favourable to liberty that he who is once found free and of free estate in a court that bears record shall be holden free for ever'? This was said because his client had once won a *mort dancestor* case, to plead in which he must have been deemed free. It could not seriously be said as an axiom that the law was always favourable to liberty since without the law

26

the shackles of servility could hardly have been fixed on the villeins. But the expression of opinion is interesting and not isolated. When the commune of Bologna emancipated the serfs of its *contado* in 1256, the book called the *Paradisus*, in which the names of masters and serfs were entered, had a preamble that serfdom was due to the fall of man, freedom being man's natural condition, and Bologna the home of freedom. Very shortly after the case of *Thorne* v. *Pecche* a preamble to the enfranchisement of crown serfs in France in 1315 stated that every man, according to the law of nature, should be free, but, much to the king's displeasure, many of the common people had fallen into the bonds of servitude. And in fifteenth-century Catalonia it was the lawyers rather than theologians who were providing an ideological basis for the rebellion of the servile tenants, the *remensas*.[1]

But the courts of King's Bench and Common Pleas do not provide as much evidence as do the records of the High Court of Parliament for the reactions of the lords in the fourteenth century. The gathering of the Commons was above all a gathering of lords of manors, and their feelings about the manœuvres of villeins to acquire freedom come out in both individual and common petitions. They complain for instance that neifs are impleading their lords in counties other than where they were born, so that the lords cannot stop their cases by counter-pleading with the writ *excepcio villenagii*. *Excepcio villenagii* was used to prove that a plaintiff was the defendant's villein and there-fore not allowed to plead. The lords reckoned that if the case came up where the plaintiff's origin was not known they would lose their man, because he would be recognised once and for all as free by a jury of his aiders and abettors. The royal reply to a petition in 1347 gave the lords (as defendants) the right to have the inquest taken in the neighbourhood of the plaintiff's birth-place. What this implied was shown by a petition of the same year which may have been connected with this ruling. A merchant of Norwich, Richard Spynk, said that the Bishop of Ely had ordered

[1] *Year Book of Edward II* (Selden Society) I, pp. 11–13, XII, pp. 121–3, XVII, pp. 144–62; R. H. Hilton, 'A Thirteenth-Century Poem about Disputed Villein Services', *E.H.R.* LVI; Luigi Simeoni, 'La Liberazione dei Servi a Bologna nei 1256–7', *Archivio Storico Italiano*, no. 397; M. Bloch, op. cit. p. 132, also quoting similar con-temporary formulae; J. Vicens Vives, *Historia de los Remensas* (1945) p. 45.

his retainers to prevent him from taking his merchandise out of the city to his damage of more than £1000. He further alleged that the Bishop had delayed a trial of the case, with Spynk as plaintiff, before the justices of *oyer and terminer* in Norwich. The Bishop also petitioned, alleging that he was being persecuted by his villeins of Doddington (Cambs.) who were getting writs of *oyer and terminer* against him in Norfolk. He wanted to deal with Spynk by a writ of *excepcio villenagii* in Cambridgeshire. Spynk said that the Bishop's power in Cambridge was so great that he would get no justice there since all men of *value* (that is liable for jury service) were either the Bishop's tenants or his paid retainers. The Bishop denied this and the King in Parliament ordered the *excepcio villenagii* to be tried in Cambridge.[1]

Joint action by manorial lords culminated in a common petition in 1377, illustrative perhaps as much of their state of mind as of the discontents of the villeins. It was alleged that villeins and tenants in villeinage were being advised by certain persons to get copies of the relevant portions of 'Domesday Book' concerning the manors where they were villeins, and that they were being further advised not to do any services on the grounds that they were discharged from all forms of serfdom whether of body or of tenure. This seems to be a reference to attempts to claim the rights of tenants on manors of the ancient demesne of the Crown. Such claims, as we have mentioned, fell short of a demand for full freedom,[2] and here the villeins are in fact accused of going much further. They were further stated to be resisting the lords' officials, threatening them with death should they dare to distrain on their property in order to force them to do their due services. The result, say the petitioners, is that the harvest is uncut to the great loss of the lords. The petitioners then hold out the alarming prospect of civil war, or aid to an invading enemy, if these rebellious elements are not crushed, for they have already collected expenses to pursue their cause and some are already at court ready to plead. The King is asked to take quick action against the villeins and their advisers – so as to avoid the peril of an alliance between villeins against their lords, such as

---

[1] *Rotuli Parliamentorum* (Record Commission, 1783) II, pp. 180*a* and *b*, 192*a* and *b*.

[2] Cf. the remarks of Justice Inge in 1315, *Year Books*, XVII, pp. 144–62.

had recently been seen in the kingdom of France (presumably the Jacquerie of 1358).[1]

Those who petitioned in 1377 must have felt that their fears were justified by the events of 1381, when, as we have emphasised, freedom was at the forefront of the grievances, and, of course, of the remedies offered, as a manœuvre, by the government. After the defeat of the rising and its immediate aftermath, parliamentary petitions continued, now stressing principally the concern of the lords that villeins were evading them by moving into towns whose franchises protected them from recapture. This reflects the great mobility of the rural population at the end of the fourteenth century, due, as we shall see, to many causes. But petitions reflecting the same sort of concern about villeins obtaining free status almost entirely die out in the fifteenth century. The main preoccupation of the classes represented in Parliament, as far as the social order was concerned, was rather their helplessness in face of the demands of wage-labourers. Indeed this preoccupation had been very much to the fore ever since 1350. Moreover, the problems of villeinage and of the control of labourers were by no means unconnected.

The interpretation which has been generally accepted of the end of villein servility is that which closely relates it to the commutation of labour services and the dissolution therefore of the close tie between the dependent tenures and the manorial demesne. T. W. Page's pioneering monograph entitled, in English, *The End of Villeinage in England* (1900) originated in a German thesis with the title *Die Umwandlung der Frondienst in Geldrenten*, that is, the 'commutation of labour service into money rent'. P. Vinogradoff in his *Villeinage in England* (1892), in spite of the many nuances in his description of villein conditions, clearly considered labour services to be the basic feature of villeinage and commutation to be the crucial factor in ending it. This view was repeated by E. P. Cheyney in 'The Disappearance of English Serfdom' in 1900.[2] But the discussion among historians concerning the tempo, geographical location and

[1] *Rot. Parl.* III, p. 21*b*.
[2] *E.H.R.* xv. Attention may be drawn to two attempts to sum up the commutation controversy, those of E. Lipson in *The Economic History of England*, I (1937) pp. 87 ff.; and of E. A. Kosminsky, op. cit. pp. 172 ff.

reasons for the commutation of labour services, though relevant to our theme, is not as central to it as some would think. It has already been mentioned that neither *servage* nor *vileinage* in France was causally linked to the performance of labour services on the demesne. In parts of England, such as the sparsely populated and economically backward north and north-west, there was plenty of serfdom without labour services even in the thirteenth century when these were generally at their height. We have already argued that, in the twelfth century and earlier, customary tenants owing labour service were probably free in public law. The connection between labour services and villein servility was made by the landowners as a matter of deliberate policy in the late twelfth and thirteenth centuries, because they wanted to guarantee an abundant demesne labour force so as to increase cash incomes through production for the market. This is the reason why, as investigations into the connection between the commutation of services and production for the market have shown, labour service used in lords' demesnes lasted longest where there was a combination of market pull and landlord control of the situation, that is in the south and south-east of the country. It is true, of course, that landlords had tended to maintain the theoretical apparatus of the labour-service system, organising various forms of temporary commutation while in practice using hired labour for most of the work done on the demesne. Labour services most called on were boon works during peak periods of sudden labour demand, when weather conditions required quick mobilisation to get the hay or corn in. Many of these boon workers were in fact free tenants.

The essence of free status and tenure was not freedom from the acquittance of rent in the form of labour service, though the labour discipline required for enforcing unwillingly performed services must have made forced labour seem, for many a villein, a very important element in his servitude. In a peasant society the fundamental freedom, obviously enough, was the right of the peasant, if not to the full product of his labour, at any rate to enough to sustain a traditional standard of living. But any medieval peasant knew, of course, that his surplus product was going to be taken away bit by bit by landowner, by lord, by Church and by State. Therefore the further freedoms which were needed were those which would limit the demands of these outsiders, make it possible to escape them or make them less burdensome in terms of the peasant's income. An important attraction of English free tenure was that an increase in services could be appealed against in the public courts. An important aspect of free status was that a free man could increase or reduce the size of his landed holding by buying and selling according to his family's needs and his own capabilities. Another was that he could sell up and get out – or threaten to do so. Freeholders also had a more secure access to common rights than customary tenants, and this meant not only pasture rights but (as the demands of villagers on the St Albans estates in 1381 indicate) access to fisheries and hunting grounds. And if he got beyond the stage where his main worry was to keep himself alive, and thought in terms of profiting by selling for the market, all these things – freedom to accumulate, freedom to build up an inheritance, freedom to dispose of his marriageable daughters – would still be of importance.

The question we must ask therefore is 'to what extent, when and how did the villein tenants of late medieval England acquire the advantages usually associated only with free tenure and status?' What we do not have to ask is 'when were villeins made into free tenants?' For manumissions, though not infrequent, were not sufficiently numerous to affect the situation of the villein class as a whole. And as John Smyth, the seventeenth-century historian of the Berkeley family wrote, 'the laws concerning villeinage are still in force, of which the latest are the sharpest'.[1] Villeinage was never abolished; it withered away. It was in the fourteenth century that the withering process began, but it was an uneven process and in many areas it was long before the manorial lords faced up to the fact.

[1] J. Smyth, *History of the Hundred of Berkeley* (*The Berkeley MSS.*, III, ed. J. McLean) p. 43.

Economic and Demographic Factors
in the Decline of Serfdom

THERE is little doubt about the direction of the general long-term trend in the relationship between peasants and their lords after the middle of the fourteenth century. Rents and such incidents of villeinage as merchets and entry fines tended to fall in value. Money rent almost universally replaced labour rent. Conditions of customary tenure approached those of free tenure whether freehold or leasehold. Agricultural wages, which must have been an important element in many middling and poorer peasant family incomes, rose, particularly towards the end of the fourteenth century. On such estates as still maintained manorial demesnes worked for the lords, leasing out to farmers (often well-off peasants) became a general policy, particularly from the 1370s. A jury from the Durham Priory village of Heworth summed up the general situation in 1373: whereas before the first pestilence each tenant had a separate holding, each now had three.[1] But whilst we too must be conscious of this important change in the ratio between cultivable holdings and the number of tenants available, we must also take into account many fluctuations and cross-currents in the situation which had an important bearing on the decline of serfdom.

One of the most significant features of the post-Black Death situation was the great mobility of the rural population. It affected tenant families and labourers alike – in so far as we can separate these into different categories. As is well known, men and women left their villages in search of high wages both in agriculture and in industry. The demand for labour did not only result from the shortages caused by the Black Death, however important these may also have been. These shortages coincided with the growth in the importance of peasant holdings of a size which would demand the employment of labour additional to that provided by the family. They often contained upwards of fifty acres of arable. These were already becoming important before

---

[1] *Halmota ... Dunelmensis*, p. 121.

the end of the fourteenth century.[1] In addition it seems possible that *before* the general leasing of demesnes there was a turnover in some estates to a greater use of hired as against customary labour, again putting up the demand.[2] Whether this demand for labour was significantly increased by the development of the textile industry, especially in East Anglia and the south-west, cannot be proved. The importance of urban and industrial demand for labour in that period has been doubted. Nevertheless such prosecutions under the Statutes of Labourers as have been found, for Wiltshire and for Essex, for example, show that there was a move of former workers in agriculture to industrial villages and towns, and to a variety of non-agricultural occupations. The opportunities presented to peasants with inadequate or barely adequate holdings must have been frequently taken up. Such alternatives cannot but have had a great effect on the relations between landlords and tenants.[3]

The other main alternatives were better holdings at improved terms of tenure elsewhere. There is, of course, no shortage of corroborative evidence to that quoted from Durham which indicated a surplus of holdings to tenants. Estate accounts show large numbers of vacant holdings immediately after the first plague, the immediate consequence of the heavy mortality. But, as Miss Levett showed, for the estates of the Bishop of Winchester these vacancies were often quite quickly refilled. This has been confirmed for other manors in Wiltshire, for the manors of the Ramsey Abbey estate in Huntingdonshire, for the estate of the Cathedral Priory in Durham, for the Crowland Abbey estate in Cambridgeshire and Northamptonshire, to quote only a few cases which demonstrate the geographically widespread nature of the phenomenon. This reoccupation was, however, deceptive. By the end of the century a more permanent situation of unoccupied holdings in the lords' hands is to be seen, and this, too, is very

[1] A. E. Levett, 'Notes on the Statute of Labourers', *Ec.H.R.* IV.

[2] J. A. Raftis, *The Estates of Ramsey Abbey* (1957) p. 258. Dr I. Keil notices the same phenomenon on the estates of Glastonbury Abbey, 'The Estates of Glastonbury Abbey' (unpublished Bristol Ph.D. thesis).

[3] N. Ritchie, 'Labour Conditions in Essex in the Reign of Richard II', in *Essays in Economic History*, II; E. M. Thompson, 'Offenders against the Statute of Labourers in Wiltshire', *Wiltshire Archaeological Society Magazine*, XXXIII.

widespread geographically. In some cases this was due as much to the flight of villein tenants as to a high death-rate. The striking figures quoted from the records of the Earl of Norfolk's manor of Forncett for the years 1376–8 show a lapse of 20 to 25 per cent of sokeman holdings and of 76 per cent of customary holdings. At that time in particular, but especially after the 1370s and throughout the whole of the fifteenth century, there was a steady drift of tenants to Norwich, to the coastal towns and to some other places, many being villages within a twenty-mile radius. In the 1390s Ramsey Abbey villagers began to move around in greater numbers than ever before until, around 1400, 'the trickle of emigration burst into a veritable tide'. Not that there was a general exodus from the countryside. The situation was rather that peasant families moved around, perhaps not very far from their original homes, perhaps even just moving from one holding to another in the same village. In Thaxted (Essex), for instance, between 1348 and 1393, three-quarters of the holdings were taken up by new families, though only 60 per cent of these new families came from outside the village. In one Berkshire village between 1379 and 1394 there was a 64 per cent turnover in the names of families occupying holdings, a mobility which continued in the fifteenth century. This is found elsewhere as well. On six manors of the Cathedral Priory of Worcester there was an 80 per cent turnover of tenant family names between the beginning and the end of the fifteenth century. A study of the same phenomenon in the Sussex village of Alciston shows that between 1433 and 1489 there was a turnover of similar dimensions, only one-fifth of the tenant families surviving the fifty-year period.[1]

Not all families disappeared through migration, of course. There were the usual biological factors of no heirs, or no male heirs. But a study of any manorial court roll for the last one

[1] A. E. Levett, *The Black Death on the Estates of the See of Winchester* (1916) pp. 83 ff.; R. Scott in *V.C.H. Wilts.* IV; J. A. Raftis, *Ramsey Abbey*, pp. 251–2; F. M. Page, *The Estates of Crowland Abbey* (1934) pp. 126–7; Davenport, op. cit. p. 72; J. A. Raftis, *Tenure and Mobility* (1964) p. 153; Newton, op. cit. pp. 29–30; R. J. Faith, 'The Peasant Land Market in Berkshire' (unpublished Leicester Ph.D. thesis) p. 63; Worcestershire data calculated from cathedral priory manorial material by E. K. Vose (unpublished); J. A. Brent, 'Alciston Manor', *Sussex Archeological Collections*, vol. 106.

hundred and fifty years of the Middle Ages will reinforce the evidence which is derived from lists of tenants at different dates. A drop in land transactions between members of the same family after 1350 in Berkshire can be matched by a similar phenomenon on the Worcestershire liberty of Tardebigge (Bordesley Abbey). Everywhere there is a growth of inter-tenant land sales and leases, sometimes, of course, for the benefit of relatives whose defective title to inherit the seller or lessee might wish to strengthen, but very often with no family link, as far as one can see, existing. On the Sussex estates of the Pelham family customary tenants were not only active in devising land by the making of entails and the sale of remainders and reversions, against the custom of the manor, but the manorial administration actually helped them to do so (for a price) and provided copies of the court roll entries as evidence.[1]

This activity by peasants, most of them villeins, the legal and illegal migrations to towns and villages other than those where they were born, the transfer of lands by sale or lease to other persons than their relatives, was not, of course, a completely new phenomenon of the post-1350 period. But to minimise the great increase in these actions by pointing to, say, thirteenth-century precedents would be to deform an important development in the history of the peasantry. The situation *was* different, partly no doubt because of demographic changes but also because of the increased self-assertiveness of the peasants themselves. This self-assertiveness ranged all the way from a surprising willingness on the part of whole families simply to abandon all for a new life[2] to collective armed rebellion. It was on a scale which presented a challenge to the lords, a challenge which could be met in different ways. One way of meeting it was to meet self-assertiveness with repression as seems to have been done in the thirteenth century. The other way was to bow to change as inevitable, and to seek

[1] Faith, op. cit.; Court Rolls of Tardebigge, Worcestershire County Record Office, Box 1188/12; Clough, op. cit.

[2] A by no means unusual entry on a Gloucester Abbey Court Roll of 1412 illustrates this. It concerns fugitives from the village of Upleadon. The bailiff is instructed to seize bodily Adam Adams *alias* Candurner and his son Richard, who are in Gloucester in the cutlery trade (*in arte cultellerie*), and Margery and Joan, his daughters, who are living at Over and Lylton (Littleton?) (Gloucs. County Record Office, D936a. M.4.ml.A).

other advantages from the lord–tenant relationship when the time was propitious. As one would expect, the first reaction of the lords was repression rather than accommodation. This view was put forward many years ago by J. Thorold Rogers, first of all in his *History of Agriculture and Prices*, later in his *Six Centuries of Work and Wages*.[1] He linked his suggestion with the view, since shown to be wrong, that, before the great increase in wages after the first plague, labour service had generally been commuted. He put forward the hypothesis that, in order to beat the rise in wages, the lords tried to reimpose services and that this produced the situation which ended in the revolt of 1381. But, in spite of the partial success of his critics on the narrow front of labour services, it seems that if Rogers had written about a general intensification of exploitation he would have been on firm ground.

A recent general assessment of the relationships between the principal contending classes of fourteenth-century society, the peasants and the landowners, gives support to this wider interpretation of Thorold Rogers's views. Dr G. A. Holmes has estimated, by analysing the accounts of the estates of the higher nobility, that income from landed property in the 1370s was only about 10 per cent below what it had been in the 1340s. If the fall in the population, as seems likely, was at least three times as great as this, it would seem that a greater burden of rent and a more intensive exploitation of demesne labour was being imposed on the peasants.[2] Such burdens could, of course, only be imposed by using the various means of coercion that the landowners had at their disposal. These included the old restrictive laws of servile villeinage and the new laws designed to keep down wages and to restrict the mobility of labour.

It was suggested by A. Savine that the enforcement of the Ordinance and Statutes of Labourers unintentionally dissolved the manorial bonds by giving preferential protection to employers as against manorial lords when the latter tried to assert their seigneurial rights over villeins employed by someone else. In fact the statutes gave clear preference to the lords who had the first call on their villeins' labour. In her detailed and authoritative work on the statutes, Bertha Putnam rejected Savine's views on

[1] *History*, I (1866) p. 81; *Six Centuries*, 1903 ed. (1st ed. 1884) p. 254.
[2] G. A. Holmes, *The Estates of the Higher Nobility in Fourteenth-Century England* (1957) pp. 114–15.

the basis of a much more comprehensive examination of the evidence.[1] And, after all, except for an unsuccessful petition in 1368 by landowners who were not lords of villeins for the levying of double damages on those demanding excessive wages,[2] it seems pretty clear that the interests behind the petitions, the legislation and the court enforcements were those of the manorial lords. As we have seen, there was a lag, often a considerable time, between the commutation of labour services and the leasing out of demesnes. In any case, lords had long relied on the labour of full-time servants rewarded by wages for the bulk of the agricultural work on the demesne. Hence their interests as employers of wage labour were as great as their interests as lords of unfree men. They had used their seigneurial rights in the past to ensure a supply of cheap hired labour,[3] and now they were to use their position as justices of labourers or of the peace to attain the same object. The overwhelming majority of the justices who enforced the labour legislation were the local gentry, reinforced by a few local magnates and professional lawyers. If it was true, as we have suggested, that well-paid work for wages offered an alternative to the servile peasant which acted as a form of pressure on lords to improve the peasant's lot, the enforcement of the labour legislation, if successful, would have blocked that alternative. This would have strengthened the position of the lords as against the villeins.

Occasional evidence of conflict between rival landowners for wage labour should not persuade us that there was a conflict in principle between the users of hired and the users of villein labour. Landowners who had seigneurial rights over villeins were prepared to use those rights in this situation of labour shortage in a variety of different ways. Robert, Abbot of Meaux (1356–76) in the East Riding, removed some labourers who were his villeins

[1] A. Savine, 'Bondmen under the Tudors', *T.R.H.S.* new ser., xvii; B. Putnam, *The Enforcement of the Statute of Labourers during the first decade after the Black Death* (1908).

[2] *Rot. Parl.* ii, p. 296a.

[3] For examples of lords using members of villein families as demesne hired labourers, see *V.C.H. Leics.* ii, p. 174; 'Scriptum Quoddam', in *Historia et Cartularium Monasterii Gloucestriae*, iii (1867) p. 213; A. Clark, 'Serfdom on an Essex Manor', *E.H.R.* xx (1905). On the estates of Ramsey Abbey at the end of the fourteenth century, free men were paid higher wages than villeins (Raftis, *Ramsey Abbey*, p. 201).

from the service of some wealthy peasants in the village of Wawne. He required these labourers for his own ploughing. It so happened that their peasant employers were also the Abbot's villeins. This episode, in fact, came in the middle of a bitter dispute between the Abbot and the villein employers, who were trying to prove that they were crown villeins and so escape from the yoke of near-by Meaux. They attempted to use the Abbot's action against him, alleging a breach of the Statute of Labourers, but in the end without success. At about the same period (1360) the Abbot of Pipewell, Northants., was complaining that the Warwickshire justices of labourers were making his tenants work for other landowners, using the coercive powers of the Statute. Like the Abbot of Meaux he was successful in invoking his rights as a lord of villeins to give him priority over the labour of his tenants. In 1371 and 1375 the Prior of Durham tried to make sure that not only labourers and workmen (*laborarii, operarii*) but cottagers and tenants who had sown no grain on, or who had sublet, their own holdings, should be available for work on his demesnes. The reeve and the forester of Arley were instructed to stop all such persons from leaving the village in case they should go off and reap for anybody but the lord and his tenants. Prior claim by lords over their own villagers for harvest wage labour had of course been a matter of manorial custom for many years, but the pressure necessarily became more acute with the post-plague shortages.[1]

On the other hand some lords were prepared to exploit their rights over their villeins' labour in other ways. In 1369 the Abbot of Evesham charged a servile tenant at Talton (Worcs.) 20s 8d for permission to employ his own brother. A later example, on the same lines, which shows how long the exploitation of this type of seigneurial right persisted, comes from Broadway in the same county in 1424. A neif of the Abbot of Pershore was employed by a man whose name (Henry Walker) suggests that he might have been a fuller of cloth. The Abbot allowed Walker to have the neif's services for six years at a payment to the Abbot of 3s 6d a year.[2]

[1] *Chronica Monasterii de Melsa*, III (1868) pp. 131–2; Putnam, op. cit. pp. 217–18; *Halmota . . . Dunelmensis*, pp. 109, 127–8; W. O. Ault, *Open Field Husbandry and the Village Community* (1965) p. 13.

[2] Evesham Abbey Leases, Leigh MSS., Stratford on Avon Record Office; Public Record Office, SC 2. 210/27.

The background to these incidents was, of course, the mobility of the rural population to which we have referred, and fierce competition between all types of employers of labour, ranging from the powerful estate owners to the small master craftsmen who were warned in 1376 not to take apprentices from any township where there was a shortage of agricultural labour.[1] The Government was powerless to keep wages down indefinitely, in spite of the enthusiastic and rigorous enforcement of the Statutes. Wages of all workers rose, but it is interesting to note that the more striking increase in real wages took place after 1380. The following wage figures have been calculated in terms of wheat so as to take into account the movement in food prices.[2]

	artisans	agricultural labourers
1300–09	100	100
1310–19	109	121
1320–39	121	140
1340–59	136	148
1360–79	147	159
1380–99	190	235
1400–19	192	210
1420–39	182	200
1440–59	241	236

It must, however, be appreciated that contemporaries probably thought more in terms of wages actually paid over in money than in terms of real wages. Agricultural wages on the Winchester Bishopric estates in pence moved as follows (piece rates, quarter of grain, threshed and winnowed):

1300–19	3·85	1400–19	7·33
1320–39	4·78	1420–39	7·32
1340–59	5·12	1440–59	7·29
1360–79	6·55	1460–79	7·22
1380–99	7·22		

[1] *Rot. Parl.* II, p. 340.
[2] Figures from M. M. Postan, 'Some Economic Evidence of Declining Population in the Later Middle Ages', *Ec.H.R.* 2nd ser. II,

These figures show a less striking jump after 1380, the big rise appearing after 1360. Both sets of figures all the same suggest that to begin with wages were held down to some extent, and this may have been partly due to the enforcement of the Statute of Labourers. It also seems to be the case that there was something of an offensive against the landholding as well as against the labouring peasants. Can we say, then, that there was a general seigneurial reaction between the first plague and the 1370s, showing itself in the successful depression of wages below their natural level and in a relative increase in revenues from land? A reaction which would have its consequences in peasant unrest, culminating in the 1381 rising?

To answer this question completely to our satisfaction there would have to be a much more complete analysis of manorial documents — in particular, account rolls and court rolls — than has yet been done. There are, however, indications in existing studies that, in some cases up to the 1370s, in other cases until later, manorial administrations were pressing as hard on tenants as the manorial lords in their capacity as justices were pressing on the labourers. There is some indication in places of an intensification or a reintroduction of labour services. This apparently happened in the estates of the Cathedral Priory of Canterbury, though the trend to the reintroduction of labour services seems to have begun after the 1314–17 famine and the drought of 1325–6. Full labour services were exacted between 1340 and 1390. The archbishops, too, were introducing a stringent attitude to their tenants. Courtenay's conflict with the tenants at Wingham, who were punished for unwillingly and badly performing carting services by the imposition of ecclesiastical penance, was an echo of the earlier harshness of Archbishop Islip. This prelate, who had excommunicated John Ball (before 1366) for subversive preaching, had been faced with difficulties over services in 1356 at Otford (Kent), services which were to be refused again in 1381. At Northfleet in 1367 reaping services were enforced, though the Archbishop's agents were unable to compel their performance from all the tenants' holdings. There were similar conflicts about boon works at Methley (Yorks.) between 1352 and 1354 leading to amercement, but eventually to partial commutation. Other

pp. 233, 226. See E. A. Kosminsky's interesting comment on these figures in 'Feudal Rent in England', *Past and Present*, 7.

cases where there is evidence of the reimposition or intensification of labour services include Berkshire, Surrey and Somerset. But these indications of seigneurial reaction are not in fact the most significant.[1]

It was not, as we have emphasised, the exaction of labour services in themselves that necessarily caused most villein resentment, though the Kentish evidence shows that even light services were felt to be an affront. This one would expect when labour was particularly precious. But labour services were used as a means to increase or sustain manorial profit, and if profit could be acquired in other ways, lords would take it. Hence it was also the raising of money rents and the financial exploitation of the incidents of villeinage which caused trouble. Rents, from peasant tenures rather than from demesne lessees, were being pushed up on the Durham Priory estates after 1350. When the Abbot of Eynsham reorganised his estate after the first plague the money that had to be paid over in entry fines, new money rents and boon services exceeded the old level of money rent plus commuted services. Similarly the post-plague money 'arrentation' of holdings formerly assessed in labour services in the Ramsey Abbey estate involved a net increase in the burden on the tenants. Money rent increases are found, too, on the Beauchamp manor of Elmley Castle (Worcs.). In a Suffolk village there was a 50 per cent increase in rent between 1358 and 1388. On the St Albans Abbey estates resentment was roused by the determination of the cellarer, John Mole (1354–75), to enforce the collection of rent arrears. Of course, a general raising of rents, when tenants were in short supply, was difficult and in the long run impossible. So other ways of raising money were tried. At Elmley Castle in 1356 the homage was amerced the enormous sum of £20 for declaring a fugitive tenant to be a free man, the punishment being justified on the grounds that they had previously recognised his villeinage. A group of Evesham Abbey leases in 1368 and 1369 cannot unfortunately be used to make a comparison of rents with those of previous years owing to the lack of estate documents, but there

[1] R. A. L. Smith, *Canterbury Cathedral Priory* (1943) chap. IX; Du Boulay, op. cit. pp. 175, 183–93; Methley Court Rolls, printed as an appendix in H. S. Derbyshire and G. D. Lumb, *The History of Methley* (Thoresby Society, 1937); Faith, op. cit.; *V.C.H. Berks.* art. cit.; H. E. Malden in *V.C.H. Surrey*, II; G. Bradford in *V.C.H. Somerset*, II.

are similar indications of seigneurial harshness, such as a fine of 40*s* for permission to marry a widow tenant of a yardland, and merchet payments as high as 20*s*, such as the Bishop of Worcester was also taking from his tenants, up to 1381. The Abbot was not making stipulations, even for villein land, about the performance of labour services, other than boon works, but he was making heirs surrender their right into his hands, and reissuing sometimes to the right heir and sometimes not, with the written condition that the tenant should be *justiciabilis de corpore et catallis*. At Killerby (Durham) in 1351 tenants were being forced to work vacant holdings, and at Forncett in the 1370s tenants were paying money so as not to be obliged to take up holdings whose burdens they found too heavy. At Methley in 1351 a tenant who tried to surrender a holding because it was unsatisfactory had it put to him (presumably by the lord's steward) that he *was* satisfied. He had to get a jury to back up his claim that he was not, and the holding was relet to another without entry fine because the land was so poor.[1]

These examples are intended to illustrate the nature of the pressure which some landowners put on their tenants in the decades after the first plague. It is clear that they saw the concept of servile villeinage as being, at that stage, essential to their interests. This is well illustrated, not merely by the general declarations that were made after the defeat of the 1381 rising when the charters of freedom were revoked, but by the interesting particular application quoted by Dr Holmes from a letter to the reeve of Odcombe (Somerset) from the Council of the Earl of March in 1391, reproving him for letting a villein holding to a free man at a lower fine than another man, a villein, was prepared to pay, and instructing him not to allow any of the lord's neifs by blood, male or female, to leave his lordship, so long as there was a living for them there. For the loss of a villein was as much a form of disinheritance as the loss of land or goods.

[1] E. M. Halcrow, 'The Decline of Demesne Farming on the Estates of Durham Cathedral Priory', *Ec.H.R.* 2nd ser. VII; B. A. Lees in *V.C.H. Oxon.* II; Raftis, *Ramsey Abbey*, pp. 251–2; Elmley Court Rolls in Worcs. County Record Office 899:95; Worcester Bishopric Court Rolls, ibid. 173.92447 ff.; *V.C.H. Suffolk*, II, art. cit.; A. E. Levett, *Studies*, p. 204; Evesham Abbey Leases, see p. 38, n. 2; *V.C.H. Durham*, II, art. cit.; Davenport, op. cit.; Derbyshire and Lumb, *History of Methley*.

The efforts made to prolong servile villeinage were in the end unsuccessful. Even the reaction which was attempted in the immediate post-plague years was not systematic. Not all landlords were able to force tenants to behave as if their bargaining position was unchanged. There are plenty of examples of the falling trend in rents and other payments coming into operation soon after 1350. On the Worcester Cathedral estate, for instance, tenants were being tempted to take up vacant holdings in the immediate post-plague years by a reduction of entry fines and a substitution of a moderate money payment for an animal heriot in the terms of the letting. On this estate, as on others, holdings and portions of holdings had to be let at low money rents until such time as someone would come along prepared to take the holding at the old rent. Entry fines were reduced in Berkshire, this being an obvious way for landlords to encourage tenants, rather than by altering the customary terms of tenure. But rents per acre also began to fall eventually, from nearly 11d at the end of the 1370s in Forncett to little more than 6d by the middle of the fifteenth century. At Alciston it was from the 1390s that rents per acre began to drop. This was precisely the time when the auditors of the Duchy of Lancaster felt the economic difficulties of landlord farming seriously enough to feel impelled to put them in writing (1388). Costs were not covered by the sale of the products of demesne cultivation, the profits of seigneurial jurisdiction were faltering, rents from mills and fisheries had fallen, profits from pasturage in the Peak Forest were down, bailiffs and reeves were refusing to do their duties in return for their tenures, so that paid officials had to be used – the auditors for the most part put the blame on individuals, but the trouble was more deep-seated. The general trend of estate revenues was downwards, typified by the fate of the revenues of the big Augustinian Abbey at Leicester between 1341 and 1477 – a fall of one-third in the income from rents, of nearly a half of the income from other sources.[1]

[1] Vose, op. cit.; Faith, op. cit.; Davenport, op. cit.; Brent, op. cit.; Holmes, op. cit. p. 126; Hilton, *Leicestershire Estates*, p. 86.

The Evolution of Peasant Tenures: Leasehold

NOW servile villeinage was historically rooted in customary tenure. The new economic conditions caused two major changes in this situation. First, a large amount of peasant land was withdrawn from the area of custom and was turned into leasehold. Secondly, customary tenure itself, without being legally enfranchised, is once more found without the taint of servility and becomes copyhold, liable to be held not merely by free men but by gentry.

Leases for terms of years, for life, or at the will of the lessor, were not new, of course, in the relations between landowners and tenants. Furthermore, even when the bulk of peasant land held from manorial lords was still governed by customary rules the tenants themselves were often engaged in subletting, usually for short terms among themselves. Although it did not provoke such dire reactions as outright purchases of free land by villeins, this subletting was either forbidden by lords, or they attempted to control it. But the vetoes and attempts at control were not particularly successful, and in many villages there must have been quite a traffic in land among the tenants. This traffic, of course, involved a purely economic relationship between lessor and lessee, in contrast to the relationship between lords and peasants which involved an element of non-economic compulsion. But when lords increased the number of leases of a non-customary character, they too tended to be determined by market considerations, particularly since the rent was usually in money.

One of the obvious reasons for the increase in non-customary lettings in the late fourteenth and fifteenth centuries was that land became available to which customary rules either did not apply, or could best be let on non-customary terms. Such land came from the lords' demesnes and from lapsed tenements which remained in the lords' hands. There were many varieties of demesne lease. Sometimes the demesne was divided into small parcels and let out piecemeal; sometimes it was let out whole to the community of the villagers who might then divide it amongst themselves; in the later Middle Ages it was commonly let as a whole to single individuals or to two partners, who were quite often well-to-do peasants of villein status. This sequence of leasing policy was not invariable. At Forncett, for instance, the demesne was at first leased as a whole together with the farm buildings to two bondmen (1376–8), but after 1400 piecemeal. Much could be written about demesne leases, but, from the point of view of their influence in the erosion of customary tenure, their main features were that they were almost invariably for terms of years so that the rent and other conditions of tenure could be adjusted according to market conditions at the end of the term. The rent was not necessarily in cash since leasing lords often wished to keep the demesne as a direct source of grain and stock for their larders. In addition to the land, the live and dead stock were usually leased too, and where relevant the remaining labour services of the customary tenants.

As an example, we may quote a useful cross-section of types of demesne lease from a Coventry Cathedral estate document of 1411.[1] We are given information about the leases existing at that date, of eleven demesnes in Warwickshire and Leicestershire. The length of the leases varies as follows: eight years; twenty-two years; sixty years; fourteen years; three years; twelve years; then there are three tenancies at will; one whose duration is not specified; and one where the lord seems to be under duress – the demesne at Packington having been taken over by the tenants without any payment of rent. Other features of these leases present almost as much variety. Six leases provide for a rent in kind, five of them being fixed amounts payable by single individuals, who are named. The sixth is leased for one-third of the grain crop. The three leases at will are for money rent, and one of the farmers is stated to be a *nativus*. The lease whose duration is not specified gives no detail either of tenant or rent. And as we have seen, at Packington the demesne was not so much leased as appropriated. Individual parcels of demesne were also let at will or for terms. On the Leicester Abbey estate parcels of demesne were already leased at will, or rather at pleasure (*ad placitum*) by 1341. Later the demesnes were leased as a whole. As mentioned above, at Forncett, the piecemeal leasing came after the leasing *en bloc*. From about 1400 onwards these were leases first of all for six or seven years, later for twelve, twenty or forty

[1] Public Record Office, E. 164. XXI.

years. In 1515 the Abbot of St Peter's, Gloucester, leased the demesne of Abload (Gloucs.) to a single farmer for eighty years. But at the date of the lease the arable and meadow land was occupied by customary tenants holding various pieces by terminable leases, so the farmer had to wait until the agreements ended.

Leases of demesnes on non-customary terms were accompanied by a general development of non-customary leasing of holdings. This is so general a phenomenon that there is a danger of it occupying too prominent a place in the interpretation of late medieval peasant landholding, though of course the amount of land leased in this way varied from place to place. When George Unwin came to write about this topic for the *Victoria County History of Suffolk*, he was so impressed by the domination of six- to ten-year leasehold tenures, by the disintegration of traditional tenements, by the emergence of well-to-do tenant farmers of a modern type and by the use of wage labour on such demesnes as were still cultivated, that he referred to one place (Hawstead) in 1388 as 'in essentials a modern village'. He may be thought to be exaggerating, even for the heavily populated and industrial East Anglian counties. Certainly elsewhere customary tenure remained strong, though the importance of terminable leases is not to be underestimated. In many parts of the country short terms of various lengths between six and twelve years are found, but life terms (meaning on average twenty years) and longer terms, up to forty years, are found in the late fourteenth and early fifteenth centuries. It is difficult to see any general sequence common to different areas or estates. In Forncett the longer leases developed after 1400. In Durham life leases in the mid-fourteenth century seem to have been overtaken in importance by tenures for short terms of years (three to twelve), renewable on payment of fines. In both types of lease tenants were able to sublet (*tabernatio*). On the Pelham estates in fifteenth-century Sussex seven years was a common term both between lord and tenant and between tenant and tenant. But in the south-west, on the Tavistock Abbey estate, the trend was towards a stabilisation of leasehold terms to forty years. On this single estate there were striking variations in the proportions of leasehold to other forms of tenure. On the whole, there was probably a general tendency towards the end of the fifteenth century to long leases, acquired by the payment of considerable fines. These varied, of course, according to the length of terms, the annual rent and other largely economic factors.[1]

Copyhold and Customary Survivals

CUSTOMARY tenure remained strong. The development of various forms of leasehold in demesne and tenant land may have had an importance greater than the amount of land in such tenure would at first suggest, perhaps as a back door to free status for those peasants able to pay the required entry fines. But in fact as customary tenures were turned into copyhold, as was general by the beginning of the fifteenth century, the servility associated with them seemed, at any rate in some places, to melt away. The possession of a deed implying a contract between landowner and tenant was thought by some servile tenants as early as the thirteenth century to make them free (*Nativus qui tenet aliquam terram per cartam incontinenti dicit se liberum*),[2] so the issue to customary tenants of a copy of the entry on the court roll recording their tenure no doubt gave the feeling of the freedom of a contractual relationship between lord and man. This was accepted on some estates. In the late fifteenth century references to the servility and bondage of copyhold disappear from the court rolls of Ramsey Abbey. After 1440 the distinction between serf and non-serf on the Pelham estates no longer mattered. In Berkshire the hallmarks of villeinage lasted during the first half of the fifteenth century, and then disappeared as tenants paid to convert their villein holdings to life-tenures. Life-tenures in fact become very widespread on customary land, without the lords at first dropping the use of the term 'customary' to describe the form of the letting. As is well known, by the middle of the fifteenth century common law was beginning hesitantly to protect the security of copyhold tenure, as were the courts of equitable jurisdiction, another indication that customary tenure was being regarded as simply one among many ways of holding land without reference to the legal and social status of the tenant. After all, the well-known legal family, the Stonors of Oxfordshire,

[1] See the works on these regions already cited.
[2] Cited by Finberg, op. cit. p. 251 n.

were not ashamed to hold copyhold land. Bishop Latimer's yeoman ancestors were probably copyholders.

The full title of copyhold was, of course, 'tenure by copy of the court roll according to the custom of the manor'. In many cases tenants had achieved an advantageous situation for themselves by the time custom hardened. The nature of the advantages varied. In 1432 an agreement between the Prior of Binham, Norfolk, and the villagers (who had burnt the manorial records in 1381) represented a certain achievement for the tenants. In addition to getting control over the services in the parishioners' part of the priory church they got entry fines halved from 4*s* to 2*s* an acre, a fixed rate for fines on non-agricultural property (shops and messuages) and a fixing of pasture rights as exercised by the lord on the one hand and themselves on the other. Essex copyhold was reputed to be 'as good as free' with rights of inheritance, fixed fines and opportunities for subletting, either outside the court for three years or in perpetuity if done through the court. Ancient demesne manors were normally privileged, of course: the favourable conditions for the copyholders of Corsham (Wilts.) in the second half of the fifteenth century are very striking. Tenures were hereditary, alienation of land was cheap and easy, whether these were sublettings or sales through surrender to use, and the tenants chose the bailiff and the rent collectors themselves. In the fifteenth century, on the Honor of Clitheroe, customary tenants did not even have to surrender to the lord in the hallmoot when they sublet, which they could do for any period. Alienation was easy, and inheritance was guaranteed. Their holdings were, in fact, 'practically as negotiable as freeholds'. In Sussex transactions between customary tenants were often made outside the manor court. At Erdington, in Warwickshire, although the succession to holdings and their alienation was recorded on the court roll, the process of surrender and reissue hardly ever seems to have occurred, even in the fourteenth century. The lord of the manor got a heriot but there were no fines for entry. A typical fifteenth-century entry shows an alienation of land to a group, probably of feoffees, by virtue of which the lord had a heriot *secundum consuetudinem manerii*, which was negotiated between the alienor and the steward, and was paid in money.[1]

[1] In addition to works already cited, see F. B. Burstall, 'A Monastic Agreement of the Fourteenth [*sic*] Century', *Norfolk Archaeology*,

But the situation did not develop evenly. Nor was the uneven development away from servile villeinage determined simply by regional differences. One has the impression rather, that it was the balance of forces between lord and villein from estate to estate, even from manor to manor, which decided how quickly villeins would become free copyholders. On the Duchy of Lancaster manor of Ingoldmells (Lincs.), in a part of England where there was much free tenure, there had been in the late fourteenth and fifteenth centuries a traffic in land between tenants especially through the device of surrender by one tenant to the use of another.[1] In other words there was considerable freedom in practice for peasants to build up their landed holdings. But as late as 1492 the court rolls record a bondwoman paying leyrwite – a mark of serfdom if ever there was one. The Canterbury Cathedral estates in Sussex may have had more serfs on them than there were in free Kent, but serfdom was not all that heavy. Yet late in the Middle Ages the prior was being tipped off to take the savings of bondmen at Blakham on the grounds that whatever a serf acquired he acquired for his lord. At Methley in 1465 the manorial jury was being fined for failing to report various delinquent villeins, such as one who put his son to school without permission and another who was living outside the lordship. Only a few years earlier (1458) a man's holding was seized because he had deflowered a neif by birth (*nativa de sanguine*).

It is possible that the apparently uneven survival of neifty by blood (or birth) was due to the unevenness of recent rural mobility. *Nativi de sanguine* of late medieval manorial documents were probably not surviving representatives of Anglo-Saxon slavery, but rather members of those few villein families who had been in the village before 1350. It is also possible that the incidents of serfdom were preserved longest where they had been established earliest and most firmly. Elmley Castle, chief manor in Worcestershire of the Earldom of Warwick, had been manorialised by the

XXXI, pt. II; A. Clark, 'Copyhold Tenure at Felstead, Essex', *E.H.R.* XXVII; N. MacNunn in *V.C.H. Essex*, II; Tupling, op. cit. pp. 74–5; *The Tropenell Cartulary*, ed. J. S. Davies (Wilts. Archaeological and Natural History Society, 1908); Erdington Court Rolls, Birmingham Reference Library, Manorial MSS. no. 347858.

[1] W. O. Massingberd, *The Ingoldmells Court Rolls* (1902).

Church of Worcester in pre-Conquest times. We find here, as elsewhere, in the second half of the fourteenth century an increase in leases for life and term of years, and opportunities for inter-tenant deals such as surrenders to use and the sale of reversions. A claim by a reversioner in 1412 was proved by the production in court of his copy of the court roll, so perhaps copyhold tenure was on its way. But the lord does not seem to have been willing to see serfdom by blood disappear. A man and his son who were *nativi de sanguine* had to pay 20*d* in 1444 for permission to stay for five months in a village hardly ten miles away. In 1478 the relatives of a neif living in near-by Pershore were ordered to bring him in under a penalty of 20*d*. Merchet was being paid in 1495 and 1498, and neifs by birth are still referred to in 1509. This is true of the Bishop of Worcester's estate also, where in 1503 a man described as a *nativus domini de sanguine* was taking a customary holding of half a nook at the high entry fine of 10*s*. In contrast, at no distance from either Elmley Castle or from the Bishop's manors on the outskirts of Worcester, there was another manor for which we have a continuous series of court rolls. This was the so-called liberty of Tardebigge, a Feckenham Forest manor of Bordesley Abbey. Life for the peasants here was no doubt hardly idyllic, holdings were small, and the Abbot was still trying to get boon works in 1460. But although tenures are described as customary throughout the Middle Ages, there is no hint of servile villeinage, and the number of surrenders by one tenant for the benefit of another (*ad opus*) suggests a fair degree of unrestricted land transactions between tenants.

Judging by transactions in court rolls of the fifteenth century, customary tenants whose servility was insisted upon did not necessarily have to pay higher rents or entry fines than free men taking copyhold land, though they still had to pay to marry off their daughters or live out of the manors. One reason why lords insisted in the fifteenth century on maintaining the institutions of serfdom was no doubt because of deeply rooted ideas about social status – the same system of ideas about status which also affected peasants who wanted freedom, even if it gave no immediate economic advantage. The social conservatism of the lords is expressed in the oath which mid-fifteenth-century Spalding Priory bond tenants had to swear when taking up holdings whose labour services and tallages had been commuted for fixed money rents: 'I xall fayth bere to the lord of this lordeschep and justi-fyable be in body, godys and in catell as his own Mann at his own wyll. So helpe me God alle the holy doom and be this boke.' The other point of view was expressed by an elderly bondman of the Abbot of Malmesbury in the 1430s who wished to be free before he died, and his heirs and blood after him, 'and if he might bring that aboute it wold be more joifull to him then any worlelie goode'.[1]

The Last Profits of Serfdom

BUT the fifteenth-century aristocracy was also nothing if not money-conscious. If servile villeinage was becoming meaningless as an attribute of peasant tenure, there were still other ways by which servile birth could be exploited financially. This could be done in the first place by manumitting a serf for cash, though such an act would have the disadvantage of removing the serf from the possibility of further exploitation on account of his status. Individual manumissions of course are found at least as early as the twelfth century, but in the days of financial difficulty for lords mass manumission was probably the best way of raising cash. The kings of France had already tried this at considerable immediate profit to themselves as early as 1246 and Elizabeth I was to have a final fling in 1575. In England there are indications of a mass manumission of the bondmen of the manor of Stratfield Saye (Hants) in 1364 for £55, but most evidence is of individual manumissions, and there is not enough of this to indicate more than that the sum paid must normally have made this road to freedom possible only for the wealthiest villeins.[2]

Sums paid for manumission also varied considerably, suggesting that they were fixed by individual bargaining. In 1317 a promi-nent aristocrat, Sir John Botetourte, was trying to recover the very large sum of 50 marks promised for an individual manu-mission. A manumission by Worcester Cathedral Priory in 1335

[1] W. O. Massingberd in *V.C.H. Lincs.* II; I. S. Leadam, *Select Cases in the Star Chamber*, I, p. 127.
[2] M. Bloch, op. cit. pp. 65–9; I. S. Leadam, 'The Last Days of Bondage in England', *Law Quarterly Review*, IX; *C.P.R. 1361–4*, p. 509.

brought in £20. A neif of the manor of Oddington (Gloucs.) paid his lord, the Archbishop of York, £6 13s 4d for his freedom in 1414. At about the same time villeins on the manors of Ramsey Abbey were paying £10 and £20. The Malmesbury Abbey villein referred to above had to borrow £10 from another husbandman for his manumission. A complicated arrangement at Egginton (Derbys.) in 1444 shows a manumission sold relatively cheap, for £3. But a squabble about a manumission promised and then delayed by the Prior of Ely, in 1465, reveals that the price was set at £10.[1]

There were other ways of profiting from villeinage without ending it by an act of manumission. One of the most striking episodes in the financial exploitation of villeinage in the fifteenth century is very well known.[2] It occurred in the Wiltshire village of Castle Combe, a centre of cloth manufacture grown up within a traditional social framework where clothiers as well as husband-men were of villein status. One of these bondmen, William Heynes, who died in 1434, was a clothier of considerable wealth. This was investigated by the Council of the lord, Sir John Fastolf, well known as a keen man on money matters. They estimated his movable goods at 3000 marks (ten times the amount calculated by a local jury), and the widow had to pay £140, compounding thus for heriot, entry fine and the right to remarry. In this case the lord had the villeins in the palm of his hand, and must have known as much as anybody about the wealth of the clothiers since he himself put important orders for cloth to them. In most other cases about which we know from the records of the courts, the prosperous villeins – or ex-villeins – were not to hand. They had removed themselves to other villages or towns. Migration to the towns had, of course, been the main feature of urban population growth for two or more centuries. To this movement was added the increased inter-village mobility which we have already noticed. So after the end of the period of

---

[1] *C.P.R. 1313–17*, p. 678; Vose, op. cit.; Gloucs. County Record Office, D621. M.7; Raftis, *Ramsey Abbey*, pp. 284–5; *C.C.R. 1441–7*, p. 215; W. P. Baildon (ed.), *Select Cases in Chancery* (Selden Society, 1896) no. 146.

[2] Documents published by G. P. Scrope, *History of the Castle and Barony of Castle Combe* (1852) pp. 223–6; further comment, among others, by E. M. Carus-Wilson, 'Evidences of Industrial Growth on some Fifteenth-Century Manors', in *Essays in Economic History*, II.

social upheavals, which was prolonged into the nineties of the fourteenth century, the pursuit of wealthy villeins became one of the main ways by which the lords could make money out of the villein condition.

To begin with, of course, the obvious hunting ground for ex-villeins would be the towns where, particularly before the expansion of rural industry, there would be the greatest concentrations of moneyed wealth. An interesting early case, a fiasco as it happened, was in 1308 when the bailiff of Sir Robert Tony imprisoned Simon of Paris, a free citizen of London, on a visit to his native village of Necton, Norfolk – or as Tony's attorney called it, his 'villein nest'. Paris (who probably got his surname by marriage into an old London family of that name) had been a citizen for ten years, had been sheriff in 1302–3 and had been a City chamberlain and alderman. He was a mercer and, no doubt, rich. On visiting Necton he had been offered the post of reeve, the acceptance of which would be a proof of villeinage, and which he refused. The case dragged on for four years. Although he had villein relatives in Necton, owing merchet and tallage, his captors could not prove that they were seised of him as a villein when he was arrested. They had to pay £100 damages. The Bishop of Ely's attempt to establish the villeinage of Richard Spynk, merchant of Norwich, in 1347, to which we referred above in another context, would be no more motivated by the wish to reintegrate the victim into the rural community than was the earlier capture of Simon of Paris. It was an attempt to make a quick profit, and so, no doubt, were other attacks on Londoners. Such, one suspects, was the background to an order sent in 1400 to the Abbot of Chertsey by chancery, instructing him not to molest or imprison Thomas Stanes *alias* Smyth, whom he claimed as his villein. Smyth's mainpernors for legal proceedings were a group of London vintners. Common petitions to Parliament in the late fourteenth century complaining about villein flight to urban franchises and especially London were no doubt mainly a reaction to the contemporary mobility of the rural population, but it may have occurred to some of them too that there would be other advantages in weakening the protection of urban custom.[1]

[1] *Year Books of Edward II*, pp. 11–13; *C.C.R. 1399–1402*, p. 175; *Rot. Parl.* II, p. 319*b*; III, pp. 212*b*, 296*b*, 448.

On the Sussex estate where the distinction between free and villein tenures was ceasing to be relevant in the fifteenth century, all the same letters of pursuit were being sent out for serfs who were outside their manor of birth.[1] Some victims were townsmen, but by no means all. We have an example from a milieu which reminds us of Castle Combe. John Kyngesson, a dyer ('litster') of Wainfleet in Lincolnshire, in 1410 was imprisoned for nearly six months by the guardian of Gilbert Umfraville, lord of the manor of Friskney, Lincs., who claimed him as a neif of that place. The sheriff seems to have been reluctant to replevy, on court order, the cattle and other chattels belonging to Kyngesson and it was not until 1413 that a second order to proceed to judgement was sent. Since Kyngesson was claiming £200 damages it would seem that he considered himself a person of some consequence. Another example of a well-to-do sufferer comes from the records of the court of chancery between 1443 and 1450. John Wayte, lord of the manor of Lee on the Solent, Hants, imprisoned John Bishop of Hamble le Rice and confiscated cash, plate, cloth and household goods valued at over £100, some of it belonging to another person but in his keeping. In justifying this confiscation Wayte said that Bishop, like his ancestors, was a villein appertaining (*regardaunt*) to his manor of Lee, and that therefore he and his heirs had 'alle maner auauntage to seise and claym the same John Bysship and his heires and theire blode, alle theire landes and tenementez, godes and catallis. . . .'[2]

A late example of the exploitation of wealthy peasants of supposed villein status comes from the records of the court of Star Chamber. Robert Carter, a tenant of the Abbot of Malmesbury in 1500 petitioned the Chancellor against the action of the Abbot who had had him arrested and imprisoned him as a bondman, ostensibly 'because the seid Robert wold not be justified by the seid . . . abbot'.[3] But the goods confiscated suggest a more practical reason: they were (according to the plaintiff) five bullocks, ten cows, nine calves and 109 sheep, the Abbot himself admitting to the same number except that he only acknowledged the

[1] Miss Clough, op. cit., gives example of four families.
[2] *C.C.R. 1409-13*, pp. 42-3, 127, 136, 179,; and *1413-19*, p. 43 Baildon, *Select Cases*, no. 139.
[3] Probably 'justiciable' rather than 'controlled' as suggested by I. S. Leadam, *Select Cases in the Star Chamber*, I, p. 123, n. 5. See the oath sworn by Spalding Priory tenants above, p. 51.

impounding of fifty-three sheep and eight lambs. This amount of livestock – not necessarily the whole of the plaintiff's possessions – already indicates a man of reasonable prosperity who could be made to buy his freedom with a substantial fine. It is possible however that the Abbot lost his case, for aged witnesses came to testify that Carter's grandfather had indeed bought a charter of manumission from the Abbot's predecessor which Carter accused the Abbot of misappropriating. Another late example of an attack on a wealthy man alleged to be a villein suggests perhaps mixed motives. Richard Hartopp of Burton Lazars in Leicestershire was, it would seem, a wealthy grazier, assessed in the 1524 subsidy on £30 worth of goods more than anyone else in the village. His particular style of husbandry brought him into conflict with two local landowners in 1520 when he broke their enclosures and pastured his animals on their grass, and with three esquires and two gentlemen in 1533, when he did the same to them. In 1536 he was evading the tithe owner by moving his sheep from field to field so as to prevent tithe lambs being taken. It was no doubt his wealth, and perhaps some lack of popularity among the gentry, that prompted Thomas Sherard of Stapleford to declare him a bondman and to try to extort his goods from him by force. Sherard cannot have hoped to bring Hartopp into his power, and in fact the Hartopps eventually acquired the greater part of the lordship of Burton Lazars.[1]

The Equivocal End of English Peasant Serfdom

IN some respects then, servile villeinage in England ended up with a number of acts of banditry by lords of manors against former villein tenants, or against those whom they claimed as such. The importance of villeinage in sixteenth-century England is a very doubtful matter. It was sufficiently present in men's minds as a condition of shame for Kett and his followers in 1549 to ask 'that all bond men may be made free, for God made all

[1] I. S. Leadam, op. cit. pp. 118 ff.; G. Farnham, *Leicestershire Village Notes*, I (1929) pp. 264–5 and V (1931) p. 374.

free with his precious blood shedding' and for a man at Ingoldmells in 1568 who called another 'a theef, and a villayn and a blood –' to be fined 16s, with 2s costs for trying to deprive the plaintiff of his good reputation and name. Queen Elizabeth's famous grant to Sir H. Lee in 1575 first of 200 crown bondmen, subsequently of another 100, for compulsory manumission, shows that bondage had some important survivals, particularly since the bondmen, mostly rather wealthy tenants of not inconsiderable amounts of land, had to pay a third of the value of their lands and goods. On the other hand social analysts of the period either minimise or deny the existence of serfdom in the England of their day, as E. P. Cheyney has pointed out. Sir Thomas Smith, in the section 'On Bondage and Bondmen' in his *De Republica Anglorum* (1565), discusses the historical and legal difference between villeins of slave ancestry ('villens in grosse') and those whose ancestors were simply customary manorial tenants ('villaines regardants', equated by Smith with the Roman *coloni ascripticii glebae*). But, as far as contemporary England was concerned, he says: 'Neither of the the one sort nor of the other have we any number in England. And of the first I never knewe any in the realme in my time; of the seconde so fewe there be that it is not almost worth the speaking.' William Harrison, writing in his *Description of England* in a chapter 'Of degrees of people in the Commonwealth of England' (1577), says: 'As for slaves and bondmen we have none; nay such is the privilege of our country by the especial grace of God and bounty of our princes, that if any come hither from other realms, so soon as they set foot on land they become so free of condition as their masters, whereby all note of servile bondage is utterly removed from them.' And Thomas Wilson, writing in 1600, knows only the following rural groups below the gentry: yeomen, copyholders and cottagers. He does not as much as mention villeinage, neifty, serfdom or bondage.[1]

In the most recent study of agrarian society in the sixteenth century, one of the contributors writes: 'Despite the development of capitalist farming and the virtual extinction of serfdom, the

[1] F. W. Russell, *Kett's Rebellion in Norfolk* (1859) p. 51; *Ingold-mells Court Rolls*, p. 289; Savine, op. cit.; Sir Thomas Smith, *De Republica Anglorum* (ed. L. Alston, 1906) pp. 130 ff.; *Harrison's Description of England* (ed. F. J. Furnivall, 1877) p. 134; Thomas Wilson, *The State of England* (ed. F. J. Fisher; Camden Miscellany, xvi) pp. 19–20.

structure of farming society yet remained intensely patriarchal.'[1]
Even the most superficial knowledge of the English agrarian
structure as late as the end of the nineteenth century suggests
that 'farming society' retained so strict a hierarchy of overlord-
ship and subordination, from the landowner through the tenant
farmer to the agricultural labourer, that one might have wondered
whether it mattered that legal serfdom became virtually extinct
three centuries earlier. What then is the significance of legal
serfdom in England and its disappearance, not, in fact, as late as
the end of the sixteenth century but rather a century earlier?

Generalising principally from French peasant history, Georges
Duby writes: 'Formerly class distinctions had been drawn
according to the hereditary and juridical lines separating free
men from unfree. But by 1300 it was a man's economic condition which counted most.' As will be appreciated from what
has been written here, this situation was reached probably a
century or more later in England. The English peasants were
able to take advantage of economic and demographic circumstances which were in themselves beyond their control, as they
were beyond the control of the manorial lords and the Government. But, as J. Vicens Vives has reminded us, it was not inevitable that the economic difficulties of the later Middle Ages
should result in the loosening of the bonds of serfdom. This was
precisely the time when in east Germany and in the states of
central and eastern Europe they were being tightened. It was at
the end of the fourteenth century and in the fifteenth century
that the *malos usos* were being imposed most stringently on the
Catalan customary tenants, not to be removed until after the two
wars of the *remensas* at the end of the fifteenth century. It is
therefore difficult to avoid the conclusion that in England, in
addition to the mobility and scarcity of labour, surplus of land
and shortages of tenants, such non-economic factors as the refusal
of peasants to accept the implications of serfdom and the inability
of the landowners to force them to do so were responsible also for
the favourable situation for tenants in the fifteenth century.[2]

[1] A. Everitt in Joan Thirsk (ed.), *The Agrarian History of England
and Wales*, IV (1966) p. 400.
[2] *The Rural Economy and Country Life in the Medieval West*
(1968) p. 282; J. Blum, 'The Rise of Serfdom in Eastern Europe',
American Historical Review, LXII; M. Malowist, 'The Economic and

The success of the English peasants in the fifteenth century turned out to be a very qualified one. Copyholders and lease-holders were in a strong position so long as the real economic factors favoured low rents, moderate fines, long leases and the choice by the tenant of his heir. But this situation was already beginning to change before the end of the century. Attempts in common law and equity to give all copyhold a security equivalent to freehold bear witness to the fact that the security of copyhold was under attack.[1] Landowners and capitalist farmers (especially grazier lessees) already wanted to convert arable to pasture at the end of the fifteenth century and when prices began to rise rapidly in the sixteenth century the weak points in manorial custom were sought out. Not all of the descendants of the medieval villeins went under. Some villein peasant families who were enriched during the period of land abundance and easy demesne leases became yeomen and even gentry in the sixteenth century. Otherwise the rural population, whether labourers or mere husbandmen, suffered a reversal of fortune. Nevertheless, their ancestors had won for them a definite gain. There was no question (in spite of nostalgic sighs from such as John Smyth of Nibley)[2] of the reimposition of individual legal serfdom, though this could not have been due to the tender-heartedness of the rulers. In the circumstances, when capitalist farming on the

---

Social Development of the Baltic Countries from the Fifteenth to the Seventeenth Centuries', *Ec.H.R.*, 2nd ser. XII; J. Vicens Vives, op. cit. chap. I.

[1] I. S. Leadam, 'The Security of Copyholders in the Fifteenth and Sixteenth Centuries', *E.H.R.* VIII; A. Savine, 'English Customary Tenure in the Tudor Period', *Quarterly Journal of Economics*, XIX.

[2] Smyth's remarks, already mentioned (p. 31), deserve quoting in full: 'and I conceive (which also a learned writer hath lately published) that the Lawes concerning villeinage are still in force, of which the latest are the sharpest; but now, saith hee, and that most truly in mine opinion, since slaves were made free which were of great use and service, there are grown up a rabble of Rogues, cut-purses and the like mischievous men, slaves in nature though not in lawe: And if any thinke this kind of dominion not to bee lawfull, yet surely it is naturall: And certainly wee find not such a latitude of difference in any creature as in the nature of man; wherein the wisest excell the most foolish of men by farre greater degree then the most foolish of men doth surpasse the wisest of beasts. . . .'

basis of wage labour, rather than demesne cultivation with the aid of tenants' services, was the predominant mode of agricultural production, and when a strong apparatus of public control could guarantee the payment of rent, there was no need of it. As R. H. Tawney wrote: 'Villeinage ceases but the Poor Laws begin.'[1]

[1] R. H. Tawney, *The Agrarian Problem in the Sixteenth Century* (1912) p. 46.

Select Bibliography

SERFDOM and villeinage have sometimes been the exclusive subject-matter of books and articles, but these topics have usually been dealt with, amongst other matters, in most works concerned with medieval agrarian history. Consequently a bibliography of medieval peasant serfdom could well be the same as one for the whole agrarian history of the Middle Ages. The bibliography contains the works most directly relevant to the matter in the text.

1. *European Serfdom*

Of the many works covering this topic the most useful for background reading are:

M. Bloch, articles on serfdom collected in his *Mélanges Historiques*, I (Paris, 1963).

G. Duby (trans. Cynthia Postan), *The Rural Economy and Country Life in the Medieval West* (1968), is the latest synthesis on the subject.

M. M. Postan (ed.), *Cambridge Economic History of Europe*, I (2nd ed., Cambridge, 1966), contains articles on individual countries (including England) of great importance.

L. Verriest, *Institutions Médiévales* (1946), contains some effective, though limited, criticism of Bloch's ideas.

J. Vicens Vives, *Historia de los Remensas en el siglo XV* (1945), is a classic study of the impact of the problem of serfdom on national politics.

II. *English Serfdom in the Later Middle Ages* (source material is not included)

E. P. Cheyney, 'The Disappearance of English Serfdom', *E.H.R.* xv (1900). An interesting early interpretation with emphasis on the commutation of labour services.

A. Clark, 'Serfdom on an Essex Manor 1308–78', *E.H.R.* xx (1905).

'Copyhold Tenure at Felstead, Essex', *E.H.R.* xxvii (1912). This discusses copyhold in the late sixteenth century, enshrining medieval custom.

Marie Clough, 'The Pelham Estates in the Fifteenth Century' (unpublished Cambridge Ph.D. thesis, 1957). Describes in detail estates straddling weald and lowland.

F. G. Davenport, *The Economic Development of a Norfolk Manor* (Cambridge, 1906; reprinted 1968). An important and detailed manorial study of the Earl of Norfolk's manor of Forncett.
   'The Decay of Villeinage in East Anglia', *T.R.H.S.* new ser. XIV (1900). Based mainly on Forncett records.

J. S. Drew, 'Manorial Accounts of St. Swithun's Priory, Winchester', *E.H.R.* LXII (1947). Strikingly illustrates the pressure of estate administration.

F. R. H. Du Boulay, *The Lordship of Canterbury* (1966). A very detailed description of social and economic conditions in Kent and Sussex.

Christopher Dyer, 'A Redistribution of Incomes in Fifteenth-Century England', *Past and Present*, 39 (1968). An unusual aspect of the silent conflict between landlords and tenants.

R. J. Faith, 'The Peasant Land Market in Berkshire' (unpublished Leicester Ph.D. thesis, 1962). A very original examination of changes in peasant family structure and custom in the late middle ages.
   'Peasant Families and Inheritance Customs in Medieval England', *Ag.H.R.* XIV (1966).

H. P. R. Finberg, *Tavistock Abbey* (1951). Important for social conditions in Devon.

H. L. Gray, 'The Commutation of Villein Services in England before the Black Death', *E.H.R.* XXIX (1914). An important contribution to the commutation discussion.

H. E. Hallam, *Settlement and Society* (1965). A very detailed account of the social evolution of Fenland communities to the end of the thirteenth century.

R. H. Hilton, *The Economic Development of Some Leicestershire Estates in the Fourteenth and Fifteenth Centuries* (Oxford, 1947).
   A Medieval Society: The West Midlands at the end of the Thirteenth Century (1966).
   'A Thirteenth-Century Poem about Disputed Villein Services', *E.H.R.* LVI (1942).

'Peasant Movements before 1381' in *Essays in Economic History*, II (1962), edited by E. M. Carus-Wilson.

'Freedom and Villeinage in England', *Past and Present*, 31 (1965).

G. A. Holmes, *The Estates of the Higher Nobility in Fourteenth-Century England* (Cambridge, 1957). Concerned more with landowners than with peasants.

J. E. A. Jolliffe, 'Northumbrian Institutions', *E.H.R.* XLI (1926).

I. J. E. Keil, 'The Estates of Glastonbury Abbey in the Later Middle Ages' (unpublished Bristol Ph.D. thesis, 1964).

E. J. King, 'The Abbot of Peterborough as Landlord' (unpublished Cambridge thesis, 1966). Deals with the market in free tenures.

E. A. Kosminsky, *Studies in the Agrarian History of England in the Thirteenth Century* (Oxford, 1956). An indispensable analysis of the 1279–80 Hundred Rolls.

'Feudal Rent in England', *Past and Present*, 7 (1955). A Marxist critique of views about late medieval social trends.

I. S. Leadam, 'The Security of Copyholders in the Fifteenth and Sixteenth Centuries', in *E.H.R.* VIII (1893). An important contribution by a legal historian. Emphasises reality of security.

'The Inquisition of 1517', *T.R.H.S.* new ser. VI (1892), discusses copyhold security with reference to early enclosure.

'The Last Days of Bondage in England', *Law Quarterly Review*, IX (1893), describes Elizabethan manumissions.

A. E. Levett, *The Black Death on the Estates of the See of Winchester* (Oxford, 1916). A fundamental, though disputed, interpretation.

Studies in Manorial History (Oxford, 1938). Contains a detailed analysis of conditions in St Albans Abbey estates in the fourteenth century.

'Notes on the Statute of Labourers', *Ec.H.R.* IV (1932).

E. Miller, *The Abbey and Bishopric of Ely* (Cambridge, 1951). Important for the position of the peasants in the East Midlands before the fourteenth century.

K. C. Newton, *Thaxted in the Fourteenth Century* (1960).

J. F. Nichols, 'An Early Fourteenth Century Petition from the Tenants of Bocking to their Manorial Lord', *Ec.H.R.* II (1930).

F. M. Page, *The Estates of Crowland Abbey* (1934).

M. M. Postan, 'The Chronology of Labour Services', *T.R.H.S.*
4th ser. xx (1937). An important article stressing the disintegration of the demesne in the twelfth century.

'Some Economic Evidence of Declining Population in the Later
Middle Ages' *Ec.H.R.* 2nd ser. II (1950). A more general
survey of social conditions than the title implies.

'The Famulus: The Estate Labourer in the Twelfth and
Thirteenth Centuries', supplement no. 2 to *Ec. H.R.* (1954).

(ed., with C. N. L. Brooke), *Carte Nativorum* (Northants.
Record Society, xx, 1950). The introduction contains important observations on the peasant land market.

B. Putnam, *The Enforcement of the Statute of Labourers during
the first decade after the Black Death* (New York, 1908). An
indispensable work with a large appendix of documents.

J. A. Raftis, *The Estates of Ramsey Abbey* (Toronto, 1957). An
analysis with a statistical emphasis.

Tenure and Mobility (Toronto, 1964). Based on Ramsey Abbey
documents, and concentrating on peasant conditions.

N. Ritchie (*née* Kenyon), 'Labour Conditions in Essex in the
Reign of Richard II', in E. M. Carus-Wilson (ed.), *Essays in
Economic History*, II (1962).

J. T. Rogers, *A History of Agriculture and Prices in England*.
The medieval volumes (I–IV, 1866–82) contain not only
statistical material but many shrewd comments by a pioneer
of economic history.

A. Savine, 'English Customary Tenure in the Tudor Period',
Quarterly Journal of Economics, xix (1905).

'Bondmen under the Tudors', *T.R.H.S.* new ser. xvii (1903).
Savine takes a less favourable view than Leadam of attempts
to give security to copyhold tenants.

R. A. L. Smith, *Canterbury Cathedral Priory* (Cambridge, 1943).
An important estate history, but from the estate owner's
rather than from the tenant's point of view.

E. M. Thompson,' Offenders against the Statute of Labourers
in Wiltshire', *Wiltshire Archaeological Society Magazine*,
xxxiii.

J. Z. Titow, 'Land and Population on the Estates of the Bishop of
Winchester, 1209–1350' (unpublished Cambridge Ph.D.
thesis, 1962). An admirable analysis in terms of demographic
expansion and land use.

G. H. Tupling, *The Economic History of Rossendale* (Manchester, 1927). The first chapters deal well with the relations between economic expansion and tenurial conditions.

W. Page, L. F. Salzman, R. B. Pugh (eds.), *The Victoria History of the Counties of England* (in progress). The articles on 'Social and Economic History' in earlier volumes are very varied in quality, but even the least satisfactory include useful evidence. Later policy has been to have specialist articles on agrarian history (e.g. Leicestershire, Wiltshire).

P. Vinogradoff, *Villeinage in England* (Oxford, 1892). The pioneer work in the subject, by no means superseded.

E. K. Vose, 'The Estates of Worcester Cathedral Priory' (n.d.) (unpublished economic history of an important and well-documented estate).

J. A. Wooldridge (Mrs Brent), 'Alciston Manor' (unpublished Bristol M.A. thesis, 1965). Now published in *Sussex Archeological Collections*, vol. 106 (1968).

Glossary

adventitius	immigrant.
amercement	payment to the lord of the court by a person found guilty of some trespass in order to have the lord's mercy. The equivalent of a fine in a modern court.
ancient demesne of the Crown	land which was the king's land at the time of Domesday Book.
ancilla	female slave.
assart	land won for cultivation from wood or waste.
boon work	labour service performed as a boon to the lord, voluntary in theory only. They were normally harvest services.
bordar	smallholder.
ceorl	free man in Anglo-Saxon law.
charte-loi	charter of privilege granted in France and French-speaking countries to urban and rural communities.
chevage	(French) an annual poll tax levied by the lord of a *seigneurie*. (English) an annual poll tax levied by the lord of a manor either on immigrant workers or on villeins allowed to live out of the manor, or on both.
colonus	free peasant in the earlier Roman period, virtually a serf by the late Empire.
commutation	conversion of the value of labour services into a monetary payment.
copyhold	the late medieval form of customary tenure, the copy of the court roll entry of admission to the holding serving as the tenant's title-deed.
cottar	smallholder.
Curia Regis	the King's court, used here in reference to its judicial capacity.
custumal	statement of manorial custom in England.

65

demesne	land on a manor not held by free or villein tenants but directly cultivated for the lord by an agent.
dreng	customary tenant in Northumbria.
entry fine	payment by a tenant as a condition for admission to a holding.
formariage	(French) similar to the English merchet.
free tenement	a term of wide meaning since it included tenures such as knights' fiefs, urban burgages and the holdings of free peasants.
gavelkind	customary free tenure in Kent.
heriot	payment at the death of the tenant to the lord of the best chattel of the holding (usually an animal).
homage	the body of manorial tenants who did homage to the lord for their holdings.
justices of oyer and terminer	justices on circuit commissioned to hear and complete pending cases.
leyrwite	fine paid by unchaste bondwoman, normally when discovered to be pregnant but unmarried.
mainmorte	(French) similar to the English heriot.
manor	the unit of territorial lordship, not necessarily coinciding with the village or hamlet, often but not invariably containing three elements: demesne, free tenures and customary tenures. Sometimes contained only one or two of these elements.
manumission	the act by which a lord freed a serf.
merchet	payment for permission to marry off a daughter (less frequently a son).
mort dancestor	a pleading in the royal courts, concerning claims by an heir that another had usurped his rightful succession to a free tenement at the death of the parent.
mortuary	the payment to the rector from a dead parishioner's goods of the second-best chattel.

66

multure	payment of a fraction of the grain ground to the lord of the mill, or the miller.
neif	a person servile by birth and blood (Latin *nativus, nativus de sanguine*).
pouvoir banal	(French) jurisdictional power of lord over subject.
pouvoir domanal	(French) jurisdictional power of landowner over tenant.
replevy	to return distrained goods to their owner by process of law.
servus casatus	(Latin) slave provided with a holding.
sokeman	free peasant, found in greatest numbers in the East Midlands.
tallage	an annual tax levied on unfree tenants.
toll	(Latin *tolnetum*) payment for leave to sell livestock.
villein	a customary tenant, in England regarded as unfree from the thirteenth century. The French *vilein* was always regarded as free in public law.
Weistümer	(German) statement of manorial custom.
wergild	monetary value of a man's life, varying according to social status, in Anglo-Saxon and other early Germanic laws. Used for compensation in case of killings.
yardland	a peasant holding in the common fields, usually 25–30 acres of arable with appurtenant meadow, pasture and common rights.

Index

Abingdon Abbey (Berks.), 23
Abload (Gloucs.), 46
Adams *alias* Candurner, Adam, 35 n.
  Richard, 35 n.
  Margery, 35 n.
  Joan, 35 n.
adventitii, 20
Ælfric's *Colloquy*, 14
Alciston (Sussex), 34, 43
amercements, 24, 41
ancient demesne of the Crown, 23, 25, 28, 48
ancillae, 15
Arley (Durham), 38
assart, 17, 19, 21, 23
Aylestone (Leics.), 19

Ball, John, 40
Bath, Bishop of, 23
Bedfordshire, 18, 19
Berkshire, 23, 34, 35, 41, 43, 47
Binham, Prior of (Norf.), 48
Bishop, John, 54
Blaby (Leics.), 19
Black Death, 32
Blakham (Sussex), 49
Bologna, commune of, 27
boon works, 30, 41, 42
bordarii, 13, 14
Bordesley Abbey (Worcs.), 35, 50
Botetourte, Sir John, 51
Broadway (Worcs.), 38
Buckinghamshire, 18
burgage tenure, 24
Burton Lazars (Leics.), 55
Bury St Edmunds Abbey (Suffolk), 20

Cambridgeshire, 18, 19, 28, 33
Canterbury Cathedral Priory, 40, 49
Carter, Robert, 54
Castle Combe (Wilts.), 52
Catalonia, 27
ceorl, 13
chartes-loi, 18
Chertsey, Abbot of (Surrey), 53
chevage, 18
Cheyney, E. P., 29, 56
Church, 11
Cirencester, Abbot of (Gloucs.), 23
Clitheroe, Honor of (Lancs.), 48
coloni, 10
Common pleas, court of, 27
common rights, 31, 48
Commons in Parliament, 27
commutation, 24, 29, 30, 40
copyhold, 44, 47 ff.
Corsham (Wilts.), 48
cottarii, 13
Courtenay, William, Archbishop of Canterbury, 40
Coventry Cathedral Priory (Warws.), 45
Crowland Abbey (Lincs.), 33
Curia Regis, 16, 17
custom, manorial, 35, 48
cutlery trade, 35 n.

demesne, 11, 14, 15, 16, 29, 30, 32, 44–5
Devon, 23
Doddington (Cambs.), 28
Domesday Book, 12, 13, 14, 28
Dorset, 23
dreng, 20

69

Duby, Georges, 57
Durham, 33
Durham, Bishopric of, 20
   Priory of, 20, 32, 33, 38, 41, 46

East Anglia, 18, 21, 22
Egginton (Derbys.), 52
Elizabeth I, 51, 56
Elmley Castle (Worcs.), 41, 49
Ely, Bishop of, 27–8, 53
   Prior of, 52
entail, 35
entry fine, 24, 32, 41, 42, 43, 48,
   52
Erdington (Warws.), 48
Essex, 22, 33, 48
Evesham, Abbot of (Worcs.), 23,
   38
   Abbey (Worcs.), 41
Excepcio villenagii, 27, 28
Eynsham Abbey (Oxon.), 41

Fastolf, Sir John, 52
Feckenham Forest, 23, 50
fenland, 20, 21
Forncett (Norf.), 34, 42, 43, 45, 46
France, 27, 29
   kings of, 51
freemen, free tenants, 11, 13, 16,
   18 ff.
free tenure, 17 ff.
Friskney (Lincs.), 54
formariage, 18

gavelkind, 22
Glastonbury Abbey (Som.), 23,
   33 n.
Gloucester, 35 n.
Gloucester, Abbot of, 23
   Abbey, 46
Gloucestershire, 23

Hamble-le-Rice (Hants), 54
Hampshire, 20, 23

Harrison, William, 56
Hartopp, Richard, 55
Hawstead (Suffolk), 46
Henry I, the laws of, 13
Herefordshire, 23
Hereford, Bishop of, 24
heriot, 15, 17, 24, 43, 48, 52
Herle, William de, 26
Hertfordshire, 22
Heworth (Durham), 32
Heynes, William, 52
Holmes, G. A., 36, 42
Hundred Rolls of 1278–80, 18,
   19, 21
Huntingdonshire, 18, 33

Inge, Justice, 28 n.
Ingoldmells (Lincs.), 49, 56
Islip, Simon, Archbishop of Can-
   terbury, 40

Jacquerie, 29
jurisdiction, private, 11, 16

Kent, 22
Kett, Robert, 55
Killerby (Durham), 42
King, 28
King's bench, Court of, 27
Kyngesson, John, 54

labour services, 11, 14, 15, 17, 18,
   24, 29, 30, 36, 40, 41
labourers, 29, 33, 36, 37 and n.,
   38, 40
   Statutes of, 33, 36, 38, 39, 40
   justices of, 37, 38
laboureur, 12, 13
de Lacy, 21
Lancashire, 21
Lancaster, Duchy of, 43, 49
land market, 35, 49
Latimer, Hugh, Bishop of Worcester, 48

leases, 44 ff.
  demesne, 32–3, 44–5
  life, 47, 50
  terminal, 45, 46, 50
  See also tenure
Lee, Sir H., 56
Lee-on-the-Solent (Hants), 54
Leicester Abbey, 43
  canon of, 26
Leicestershire, 18, 19, 45
Levett, A. E., 33
leyrwite, 49
Lincolnshire, 18
London, 21, 22, 53
'Lylton', 35 n.

mainmorte, 18
Malmesbury Abbey (Wilts.), 23, 51, 52
  Abbot of, 54
malos usos, 57
manouvrier, 12
manumission, 51–2
March, Earl of, 42
Meaux, Robert, Abbot of (Yorks.), 37–8
merchet, 15, 17, 19, 26, 32, 42, 50, 53
Methley (Yorks.), 40, 42, 49
mining, 23
ministeriales, 9
money rent, 32, 41, 43
mort dancester, 26
mortuary, 24
Mowsley (Leics.), 19
multure, 24

nativi, nativi de sanguine, 13, 14, 45, 47, 49–50
Necton (Norf.), 53
neifty, 14, 17, 49
Norfolk, Earl of, 34
Northamptonshire, 21, 33
Northfleet (Kent), 40

Northumbria, 20
Norwich, 27–8, 34
Nottinghamshire, 21

Odcombe (Som.), 42
Oddington (Gloucs.), 52
Otford (Kent), 40
Over (Gloucs.), 35 n.
oyer and terminer, 28
Oxfordshire, 18, 19, 23

Packington (Warws.), 45
Page, T. W., 29
Paris, Simon of, 53
Parliament, 27, 28, 29, 53
Peace, Justices of the, 37
Peak Forest, 43
Peasants' Revolt of 1381, 25, 26, 36, 42
Pecche, Bartholomew, 26
Pelham family, 35
  estates, 46, 47
Pershore (Worcs.), 50
  Abbot of, 38
Peterborough Abbey (Northants.), 21
Pipewell, Abbot of (Northants.), 38
pouvoir banal, 11
  domanial, 11
Putnam, Bertha, 36

Ramsey Abbey (Hunts.), 33, 34, 37 n., 41, 47, 52
Rectitudines Singularum Personarum, 15
remainder, 35
remensas, 27, 57
reversion, 35, 50
Rogers, J. E. Thorold, 36
Rossendale, Forest of, 21

St Albans Abbey (Herts.), 20, 31, 41
  Mole, John, cellarer of, 41